Collins discover

Birdwatching

Collins discover

Birdwatching

Rob Hume and Dominic Couzens

 Collins

An Imprint of HarperCollinsPublishers

ISBN-10: 0-00-719527-3
ISBN-13: 978-0-00-719527-5

ISBN-10: 0-06-084989-4 (in the United States)
ISBN-13: 978-0-06-084989-4
FIRST U.S. EDITION Published in 2006

HarperCollins books may be purchased for educational, business, or sales promotional use. For information in the United States, please write to: Special Markets Department, HarperCollins Publishers, 10 East 53rd Street, New York, NY 10022.

The name of the "Smithsonian," "Smithsonian Institution," and the sunburst logo are registered trademarks of the Smithsonian Institution.

Text © Rob Hume 2005
Updates for North American edition by Dominic Couzens, 2005
Photographs: rspb-images.com; FLPA; Mike Read; David Tipling/davidtipling.com (see p.190)
HarperCollins Publishers: pp.15, 26, 31
Illustrations: Lizzie Harper: pp. 45, 47

Color reproduction by Colourscan, Singapore
Printed and bound by Printing Express Ltd, Hong Kong

10 09 08 07 06
8 7 6 5 4 3 2 1

contents

Introduction

Birding is now one of the major pastimes in North America. A recent estimate by the U.S. Fish and Wildlife Service put the number of birders in the United States alone at over 50 million, and each year about 100,000 committed people take part in the National Audubon Society's Great Backyard Bird Count. That's a lot of people.

Why is birding so fascinating?

The early American birdwatchers were adventurers and collectors who sought birds for food, clothing, and decorative uses. Decades ago, many thousands of people supported wild bird conservation, and many more fed the birds in their backyards, but much smaller numbers actually went out to watch birds—in fact, the American Birding Association had only 115 members in 1969, compared to 22,000 now. So what is it about birds that grabs the attention of so many people nowadays? What is "birding" all about—what do these people do? This book tells you. There is nothing exclusive, nothing magic about it—except the birds themselves.

Watching birds can be a casual, simple matter, or it can become a purposeful activity, with an end in mind; or, for some people, encounters with wild birds can be moving or stimulating. To most birders, there is something of all three—birds can be appreciated every day, as something that adds interest to the journey to work or the view from the kitchen window, but they can, at times, become the objects of more serious, disciplined pursuit. And, now and then, there is an experience that transcends that and sticks in our memory as a magical moment.

This book will help you start turning basic appreciation into something a little more determined. It does not have to be difficult, nor do you have to learn complicated subjects. Making your birding more rewarding and giving it a purpose can start by watching the birds in your own backyard. Knowing a little more about the subject generally gives any hobby more substance and generates greater satisfaction. That is the purpose of this book: to help you get more from birds and to enjoy them to the full.

▶ People often get hooked on birding when they see great birds, such as the mountain bluebird.

getting

started

Birds are the most visible and popular form of wildlife. They are everywhere you look; you can see them from your kitchen or office window, from a car on the freeway, or at the shopping mall. Anyone who finds that birds can bring a bit of life and color to their day can be a birder; there is nothing complicated about it.

What is a birder?

There is a difference between someone who simply enjoys having birds around and a birder who wants to know more about these fascinating creatures. With the help of this book, you will learn how to make more of your interest and also how you can take it a step or two further. A passion for birding can take you along many, varied routes.

Wonderful creatures

Birds are capable of feats that people cannot come close to with the most sophisticated technology. They survive outside in all weathers, from the equator to the poles, from sea level almost to the height of Mount Everest, the highest peak in the world. Some birds can dive 100 meters or deeper in the ocean. They find their way around the globe without the aid of an external map, compass, or clock. Most of them fly well; many are masters of the air. No wonder we enjoy watching them.

Pursuing your interest

Birding involves people in photography, drawing, painting, or writing. However, you might prefer a more scientific approach, moving towards biology, ecology, and conservation. Alternatively you might want to become an expert in identifying birds, or you may go chasing strays and rarities. Some birders collect books or paintings, while others travel the world to build up their lifelists, visiting incredible places on the way. Who knows what you may choose to do?

With conservation in the forefront of public affairs and so many bodies concerned with the welfare of our natural environment, there may even be opportunities for employment in the birding sphere—the U.S. Fish and Wildlife Service would be a good place to start enquiries.

MUST KNOW

Types of birders
So long as what you do does not harm the birds, you can decide what you do about your hobby and how you do it. Some people are scornful of "ignorant" bird lovers who don't progress beyond watching their backyard, while others consider listers (birders whose preoccupation is seeing as many species as possible) to have a screw loose. But who cares? There is enough to learn and enjoy about birds to suit everyone.

▶ Many of us begin with birds that are close to home and familiar, such as the American robin, a bird that is tame, easy to see, and simple for a beginner to identify.

What do I do?

Most people notice birds from their window or in some other everyday activity, such as traveling to work, collecting the children from school, or working in the yard. Sooner or later there will be some song or call that catches your attention, or a bird that always flies up to a particular perch, so you begin to wonder what it is, or why it is there. Take care—you might get hooked.

Identifying birds

The next step, once you have noticed that birds exist—surprisingly, perhaps, many people appear not to—is to find out what they are, or which is which. Bird books have the first bit of jargon to describe this: "identification." It sounds a bit daunting, maybe even a bit exclusive, and you might think that it's not for you after all.

However, don't worry about it—identification is just a term to describe how we can tell birds apart and distinguish them from each other. It will lead you into areas of knowledge and expertise that might surprise you. Knowing what a bird is can open up new opportunities for enjoyment–finding out more will increase your pleasure in your new interest, not lessen it.

MUST KNOW

Apart from having no rules, birding does not require vast amounts of equipment. You can spend your dollars, if you wish, on the latest optical gear, cameras, and digital equipment, but you can get along with almost nothing. You will need a pair of binoculars and a fieldguide.

◀ We all know the mockingbird by its voice, but the bird itself, if it keeps quiet, is less easy for us to recognize.

Principles of Birding Ethics

The American Birding Association has produced a code of practice for its members that can be applied to everyone. In short, it makes clear that birders should respect the bird, its environment, and the rights of others. For a fuller version of this code visit www.americanbirding.org/abaethics.htm.

● Promote the welfare of birds and their environment.

● Avoid stressing the birds by exercising restraint and caution during your observation of them.

● Keep well back from nests, roosts, display areas, and important feeding sites.

● Stay on roads, trails, and paths where they exist; otherwise keep habitat disturbance to a minimum.

● Do not enter private property without the owner's express permission.

● Follow all laws, rules, and regulations governing use of roads and public areas.

● Practise common courtesy in contacts with other people.

● Feeders, nest structures, and other artificial bird environments must be safe.

Delving more deeply

You will soon find a level that suits you. If you stick at telling a cowbird from a starling, a towhee from a junco, or a kingbird from a mockingbird, that's fine. Plenty of people go little or no further yet they have a lifetime of enjoyment from the birds. However, it is more enjoyable to make progress and delve more deeply into the lives of birds and the possibilities of birding.

Sharing your enjoyment

You can learn by trial and error, which is often the most enjoyable way, if you have time, but you may never know if you are getting it right or getting it wrong. Sooner or later you will want to find someone else who knows about birds, and there are several ways to do this. Behind the development of most identification experts there is usually a knowledgeable friend. Birding can be a solitary pursuit, but it is best done with a friend who can share the excitements, give you some encouragement, and also offer different opinions if you get stuck with an identification.

Binoculars

To do much more than watching from a window, you must have binoculars. They need not cost more than $50, but the better ones will be in the range $300–500, and some will be as expensive as a birding vacation, over $1,000. Get the best ones you can afford, but don't worry if they are not incredibly expensive—many cheaper models will still give good results.

Choosing binoculars

Good binoculars will last a lifetime, so you should be comfortable with them. They should not be too heavy: A long day with heavy binoculars around your neck can be tiring. They should not be too big: You need to be able to handle them with ease, and use the focusing ring with a fingertip without changing your grip.

Porroprisms and roofprisms

Most binoculars now come in two basic types:
● Porroprisms, which have a stepped shape (the traditional type).
● Roofprisms, which look straight-sided and are generally more compact.

Porroprisms give a better 3-D impression, because the larger lenses ("objective lenses") are further apart. People with large hands may find roofprisms a little small, whereas the larger, wider porroprisms are unwieldy for smaller hands.

Roofprisms tend to be lighter, and they have a more modern optical system (of lenses and prisms) inside. However, they are not necessarily better, and they are also more expensive.

Eyepieces

These come in several shapes and sizes, and you need to be sure they are comfortable and do not allow in too much light from the side. They may be deep (good if you like to press them

▲ Binoculars are essential for a birder: but they can be a once-in-a-lifetime purchase if you can afford to buy a good-quality pair. To make sure that they suit you, try them before you buy them.

GETTING STARTED

firmly against your eye sockets) or shallow (not so good if you like to push them hard against your eyes for better stability). Some models have retractable eye cups so that they fold flat or "pop" down, which enables you to use the binoculars while wearing spectacles, with only a minimal loss of field of view. Look carefully at these: Rubber eye caps eventually wear out and may be expensive to replace, whereas "pop up" types that snap into position may be dust-traps.

▲ Birders use a great variety of binoculars, spotting scopes, and associated equipment, proving there is no single answer to what is best: A lot depends on what size and weight suit you best.

▼ The traditional-shaped porroprisms have large lenses which are set further apart than the straighter-sided roofprisms (below left). They will give a better 3-D impression.

▲ Lightweight, compact, and modern, roofprisms are comfortable to carry around.

Choosing the right specification

Decide on the magnification and the size of the objective lenses. These are shown by numbers that describe binoculars, such as 8x30 and 10x40. The first number is the magnification; the second is the width of the lens in millimeters.

Go for a magnification of 7, 8, 9, or 10. Six is a little too low; 12 or above is too high. Don't be tempted by binoculars that let you see "craters on the moon" with a magnification of 20 or so. They will be too big, probably of inferior quality, and you simply won't be able to hold them still. Vibration, your heartbeat, and trembling hands all make the image dance in front of your eyes; the higher the magnification, the worse this will be.

Also, the higher the magnification, the more light is required (thus the wider the lenses) for a bright, clear image. So, while 8x30 is okay, 10x30 will be too dull: Divide the first number into the second to get an idea of brightness. A pair of 7x50s will be really bright (7.1); 10x40 (4.0) will be less so but still better than 8x30 (3.7). Brightness is improved by the glass quality and the coatings applied to prisms and lenses, so very expensive 10x42s are likely to be beautiful to look through.

Why not go for 8x40 or smaller? The smaller magnification is not a real handicap and it gives you closer focus, a brighter image and a wider field of view. They are likely to be cheaper than a pair of 10x binoculars and of equal quality.

▲ Top-quality binoculars are expensive but brilliant, and can be a once-in-a-lifetime buy. You generally get what you pay for, but it is entirely your decision whether you think the top name makes are worth the extra dollars.

MUST KNOW

Larger lenses

The problem with larger lenses is that they make the binoculars bigger and heavier, so you have to compromise: 10x50 sounds good but they are big; 10x40 might be a better bet. Also, the higher the magnification, the further away the binoculars will focus. It is fine to have 10x50s to look out over a sewage lagoon or coast but irritating if you use them in a forest or park and have to keep backing away to get a bird in focus.

Setting yourself up

Binoculars have two focusing wheels. One is the central focus that operates both sides together, and you will use this constantly. People will sometimes borrow binoculars and say, "Don't worry, I won't change your setting," but they must see everything in a blur.

You must change the setting; the focusing wheel adjusts to the distance to the object you are looking at and, since you are watching birds, they will be moving about all the time and therefore you must adjust your focus to match. You will need to change focus more with a higher magnification than with a low one, which has a better depth of field.

The second focusing wheel, which is hidden away at one end or one side, is a wheel that adjusts the right-hand side. This wheel balances any difference between your eyes, so you can set it, as accurately as you can, once and then leave it alone. Some products will have a click-stop or lockable eyepiece setting; others have a simple twisting eyepiece and this needs checking every so often, as it may rub against you and turn round after a time.

▼ Look at the grip on the binoculars that is being used here: one hand firmly grasps the body with the fingers ready to adjust the focusing wheel, while the other uses the fingertips (together with one elbow on a knee) to offer stability.

▲ It's a good idea always to have your binoculars slung around your neck on a comfortable strap just in case you see an interesting bird. If you keep them in their case, the bird might fly off before you get them out.

Setting the eyepiece

To set your eyepiece, find something sharp and clear to look at, such as a pole or sign. Cover the right-hand lens, without getting fingerprints on it, and focus the central wheel while looking only with your left eye. keep your right eye open, to avoid strain and distortion. Now cover the left lens, uncover the right, and look with your right eye. Don't touch the central wheel now. Just adjust the right-hand eyepiece: Take it way out of focus first and then, with your eyes relaxed, bring it back until it is as sharp as you can get it.

This has balanced the two eyes, so you use only the central wheel from now on. Check the eyepiece setting every so often just to be sure; if you don't do this, you may have one eye always slightly blurred.

Look after your binoculars

Don't go out with your binoculars in their case; hang them round your neck on the strap, so that they are "at the ready." Get a broader, slightly elastic strap if they are not comfortable, but keep them round your neck so you don't drop them or accidentally swing them against a wall or post. If you have them around your neck but have to jump a creek or climb over rocks, hold on to them: They are painful if they swing up and hit you in the teeth!

Clean the lenses occasionally—blow away any dust or grit before touching them and then wipe them gently with a soft cloth. Don't use water. Most of all, keep sticky fingers off the lenses. A rain guard is useful in wet weather and also to keep crumbs and drops of coffee off the lenses if you are eating your lunch outside. Don't leave them about for a long time in the hot sun, as this may damage the lens coating. In very humid areas you may need to use desiccant, which is available from your camera store.

MUST KNOW

Useful tip
To help keep your binoculars steady, you just stick one finger against your forehead, or a thumb against your chin.

In the car, the carrying case might have some value, but the small plastic lens caps are a waste of time. Make sure your binoculars aren't likely to fly off the seat if you stop suddenly. If you've left them in the car overnight, warm them up before stepping outside on a cold day, or you may have misted-up lenses for the first 10 minutes; that may be when the best bird flies by.

Using your binoculars

This becomes easy with practice. It's important to get them on the bird quickly: Birds have a habit of flying off when you stop to look at them.

● Don't look down at your binoculars, then raise your head and swing them around until you "hit" something. Instead, bring them up to your eyes.

● Keep your head up and your eyes on the bird.

● Just raise your binoculars with your hands and put them directly to your eyes, so that you keep looking at the right spot.

● If you are waiting for a bird in a bush to pop up into view, focus the binoculars on the most likely point where it may reappear.

Keep them raised at chin height so that you're prepared for it when the bird appears—but don't breathe into the lenses and mist them up.

▼ "Fieldcraft" involves getting close to the birds without disturbing them, and then maneuvering into position to get a good view through your binoculars. Using them to their best advantage will come with practice.

Spotting equipment

A telescope magnifies things more than binoculars but you cannot "see further." With any optical equipment, you can only see exactly what can be viewed with the naked eye—it just gets bigger. On a misty day, you will just see a larger gray shape; against the light, you will see a bigger silhouette, so don't have unrealistic expectations.

Types of telescope

Standard spotting telescopes are available in two main shapes: straight and angled.

● Straight means you look straight through at the bird and that you can point the spotting scope at it relatively easily.

● Angled means you look into the eyepiece, which is not aligned with the main body of the scope. This makes finding the bird more difficult, but you can sit and look "down" into the eyepiece more comfortably, or stand and do the same, without having to bend down and crick your neck. Tilting the scope upwards to watch something overhead is far easier, as you don't have to lie down on your back to do it.

Astronomical scopes

Some birders use astronomical scopes such as Questar, Celestron, and Tele Vue. The best ones are expensive and can be tricky to use, but for clarity at high magnification, they are unmatched.

Magnification

A spotting scope can enlarge a bird 20, 30, or 40 times. However, the higher the magnification, the bigger the lens needs to be to get a bright image: 30x30 is useless, but 30x80, which is superbly bright, is big, bulky and heavy. You will have to compromise to get the best quality at the best price, with the least weight and bulk.

> **MUST KNOW**
>
> **Telescope tip**
> Always try to use the spotting scope with both eyes open. It will help reduce eyestrain, which can be a real problem if you use a scope for long periods.

▼ Tripods, as used here for supporting a spotting scope, are both solid and substantial and are ideal for cameras, too.

Tripods

The higher power makes the problems of a wobbly image much greater—somehow you will need to hold a spotting scope very steady. A nearby wall, fence, or tree might be helpful; otherwise you may have to sit down (maybe in a wet field) and balance the scope on your knee (but modern models tend to be far too short for this to work). You will almost certainly prefer to use a tripod, and this means something even bigger, heavier, and more ungainly to carry about with you all day long.

You can use a tripod with its legs closed up if you sit or kneel down; on a steep bank, you might have two legs closed up and one leg half-extended to ensure that the tripod is sitting comfortably on the bank. There are many ways to use a tripod; it does not have to be standing up with its legs fully extended.

▲ Tripods are more rigid and offer greater flexibility when just half extended, or with one leg extended to adjust for uneven ground, with the observer seated.

What to wear

There's a lot of nonsense talked about birders' clothing; people walk around popular wildlife refuges on a hot day in camouflage clothing and heavy boots, when jeans, trainers, and a T-shirt would be more practical. However, you must decide what you want to wear and you should just aim to be comfortable, to be warm or cool as desired, and to be prepared in an appropriate way for the weather conditions.

Clothing

Obviously, it makes sense not to be dressed in colors that are too bright, but a bird is likely to see or hear you before you see it, even if you are in dull green. If your face and hands are pale, they are usually a giveaway at long range. So, don't worry too much about your clothing: In any case, most people make so much noise

▼ The pale jacket stands out, but considering there are a handful of people here, in an open wood, that may not be too much of a problem. The birds will have seen them anyway.

crunching on gravel, treading on sticks, or talking to each other that any sort of camouflage clothing is not going to be of much use.

There is such a wide range of superb outdoor clothing from which to choose, including good, breathable, waterproof but rustle-free fabrics which tend to be ideal, whatever the weather.

Hats and footwear

Remember the special value of wearing a warm hat on a cold day. Most of your body heat is lost through the top of your head so a hat will keep it in. Footwear is more difficult. If you are hiking as well as birding, always be safe and wear some strong walking boots, but for everyday birding, everyday wear will usually be fine.

▲ It is important to be warm and comfortable. Wear a soft, lightweight jacket, baseball cap, and boots.

MUST KNOW

Clothing tip
Keeping dry and warm will help determine if your outing is enjoyable. Layers, layers and more layers. You can take off clothing but you cannot always put it on.

Using reference

One of the joys of many birders' lives is their bird book collection. Although you can spend a fortune on rare books, to most of us books are there to be used and are bought for their practical value. You will need a good reference book from the start if you are to learn which bird is which, let alone find out more about them.

Fieldguides

A good "fieldguide" is essential. Don't worry about the name—it doesn't mean that a "field" guide isn't for you simply because you usually watch from your window. Birding has its own language which tends to exclude a lot of people, but it should not. A fieldguide is simply a book that shows you how to tell the birds apart. Decide which one you like best and whether you prefer photographs or illustrations. Ideally, you should get one of each.

Photographs

Photographs are supposed to be "real" but all kinds of problems are associated with them, such as heavy shadows, reflected colors (any "white" bird is likely to have a range of grays, blues, and browns within its "white" plumage), and quirky shapes. Photographs can also "freeze" birds in awkward positions.

Illustrations

Illustrations can remove these irrelevancies and present the "perfect bird" in a side-on pose, with the colors perfectly shown, but this depends on the artist's skill and the quality of printing. Artists all have their own style, so their birds are not necessarily spot-on representations. It is best to buy several different illustrated guides, as well as a photographic one to supplement them.

Video and DVD guides

Videos are remarkably comprehensive and add real movement and character to the static and sometimes unrepresentative photographs of books—the problem has always been finding what you want without having to spool backward and forward. The development of DVDs, however, has put an end to this problem, and new guides are being produced all the time. They are superb supplements to the basic guidebook, but as yet you cannot take them out birding with you.

GARDEN BIRD SOUNDS

A sound guide to 70 garden birds of Britain

▲ Bird song CDs are a good way of learning to identify and distinguish between different bird vocalizations.

CDs

CDs of bird songs and calls are of wonderful quality. The arrival of the digital CD was a huge step forward in bird sound recordings, giving magnificently lifelike representations. There are a large number of good CDs commercially available, some of which cover just one state or even a single location.

Using the internet
The internet is a superb tool for birders of all kinds. From finding out some obscure facts about birds worldwide, to having your say on birding subjects during online discussions, the web has it all.

If you are seeking information about the birds themselves, the Laboratory of Ornithology at Cornell University, in association with the American Ornithologists' Union, has recently set up a subscription service called "The Birds of North America Online" which tells you absolutely everything you might want to know about our breeding species. There are also online rare bird alerts, hundreds of sites detailing how to attract birds to your garden, and, of course, dozens of retailers who take money on-line for every birder's item from books to spotting scopes. You can view libraries of photographs, discuss the minutiae of bird identification, or simply add your own sightings to the national database. The challenge is to log off and go and look for the birds yourself!

Keeping records

You may wish to keep some sort of record of what you see, and it is recommended that you do. Most of us like to know which birds we have seen, so you could easily become a lister. However, recording what you have seen does not need to become an end in itself, or make you competitive with other birders—most of us simply like to know what we have seen and what we have not.

▲ Keeping a bird diary is a good way of recording what you see. You might also like to make sketches out of doors of birds and their distinguishing features in a pocket notebook.

Keeping a bird diary

There are various ways of recording the birds you see, and a simple diary is an easy method, which has many advantages, especially if you keep it going for years. You can make a written diary on a notepad and then, as many birders now do, you can log your records and observations on to a database on your PC, together with any photographs you might have taken. You need not record birds every day—just when you see something interesting. The entries can be as long or short as they need to be.

Making entries

On your field notepad put the month in the top corner of each page, and start each entry with the day and date. Then list the birds in two, three, or four columns (one takes up too much space)—keep them in some sort of order, even if only roughly (all the ducks, then the birds of prey, then the shorebirds, and so on). You can add symbols if you like—stars for great views, underlinings for anything special, and red capitals for a bird you've never seen before. Add a little explanation at the bottom so you expand from a list to a more interesting and informative record of your birding activities.

I've done this for years. The advantage is that you can look back to any date and see instantly where you were, what you did, and what you saw, all written at the time and in the field, so it provides a marvelous record of an important part of your life. If you also enter your notes into a database, you can search for all the times you've seen a certain species, rather than having to trawl through years of diaries to find this information.

Why keep notes?

Most birders keep notes and records for their own amusement and information. We all learn from our observation and may even make useful contributions to ornithological knowledge. If we carefully note bird behavior, for example, it will add greatly to the simple lists of species and numbers. Another advantage of writing things down, especially in the field, is that it helps you to be thorough. If you are looking at an unfamiliar bird, making a sketch or description will help you remember to check details you might forget, such as the leg color or the wing pattern. But even species and numbers have value, as we shall see later in this book, and to use them, we must keep a record, somewhere. So a bird diary or computer record becomes essential.

MUST KNOW

Make notes
It is always better to note things down as you progress and become ever more experienced, than to take digital pictures and leave it at that. Such information will go "in one ear and out the other" without making much lasting impression.

▼ How often do hummers visit your feeder? Do they come every day at the same times or in any particular season? Try to work out what may be influencing their visiting patterns and make a note in your diary.

Photographing birds

Wildlife photography used to be highly specialized, expensive, and difficult. A few famous pioneers made a living from it; some made films for television. Now many people try, but relatively few make a go of it commercially. Nevertheless, the gap between the professional and the keen amateur has closed, through the introduction of top-class single lens reflex cameras, followed by the digital revolution.

Single lens reflex cameras

Pocket point-and-shoot cameras may have a zoom facility but the lens that takes the picture is separate from the viewfinder; you do not see exactly what you are taking. However, a single lens reflex camera uses a clever system of mirrors and prisms to make the light entering the main camera lens appear through the viewfinder. Only at the moment the shutter is released does all this optical gear flick out of the way to let light hit the film. You see exactly the picture you take. With interchangeable lenses, the photographer can also use long focus lenses to give extra magnification: To get "close in" to the subject.

Conventional lenses with up to 300 or 400 mm focal length give decent magnification but are big and heavy: The mirror lens, a squat, wide piece of equipment, reduces the length, if not the weight.

◀ With a single lens reflex camera and modern color films that work very fast (meaning shorter exposures are possible, even in quite dull light) and have smooth, rich colors, photographers can produce stunning results. But it still takes time, patience and skill, as well as a good knowledge of bird behavior.

Types of bird photography

There are two main kinds of bird photography: Stalking, more or less out in the open, but using whatever cover you can find; and bird blind work, using an existing structure—even your own window into your backyard, a fixed blind at a wildlife refuge, or a movable or temporary blind that you build yourself.

▲ Photographing birds is an absorbing and rewarding pastime. There are many opportunities to exercise your hobby when you are at home watching backyard birds, out for a hike on a trail, or on vacation.

Stalking

This is simply getting close to a bird by fieldcraft: Creeping through brush, even crawling along flat to the ground, until the bird is close enough to make a large image on the film. To do that, the bird has to be closer than you might think. Many people think they have got a good picture, only to be disappointed by the tiny bird in the middle of a big picture when it is developed. There is also "wait and see" photography—perhaps sitting by a pond in a forest, waiting for birds to come for a drink. Waiting at a backyard window for birds to visit a feeder is much the same, but it does give a series of repetitive images after a while.

Bird-blind work

Blinds mean more work, more preparation, perhaps the use of private land where other people will not interfere. However, a blind will give more complete cover to the photographer, although sitting for hours in a small, cramped space can be both tedious and backbreaking. The idea is to be close to the bird while it is unaware of the photographer's presence.

Blinds were traditionally placed near nests, but fortunately nest photography has long gone out of fashion—it risks too much disturbance and, in any case, rare birds can only be approached at the nest with the correct permits or licenses.

You can use a blind near a high-tide roost to get shots of shorebirds and ducks, or beside a garbage dump where gulls congregate, or by a lakeshore to get the best shots of passing loons, grebes, or coots. A blind offers immense opportunities to get close to birds—a great privilege and a wonderful experience.

Wherever they are, blinds must be used responsibly. If you get to the blind by a high tide roost an hour in advance of the birds, you may

▲ Fixed blinds at wildlife refuges can be surprisingly good, but they have the disadvantage of being open to the public. Take care not to "take over" when other people wish to use the blind. Photographers should be aware of other birders as well as the needs of the birds.

have to sit there for several hours until the tide recedes and the birds fly off. It would be wrong to get your pictures, then step out and scare the birds away after an hour. In every case, the bird photographer's motto is just like any birder's: The welfare of the bird always comes first.

Digital photography

This is no different from photography with film, except you record images on a card. You can simply wipe off the images you don't want while you are out of doors and then download the ones you do want on to a computer at home and use the card again. There is no waste of film or development costs, once you are over the initial expense of buying the memory cards.

▲ A digital camera means that you can photograph the birds you see and view them on your computer at home. You can e-mail the images to your birding friends and put them on a website.

You can e-mail pictures to friends or bird magazines, put them on a website, or organize your own files, albums, and slide shows. However, it is less easy to show your pictures to other people unless there is a computer to hand. Of course, you can print out the images as digital color prints although the quality may not be as good as traditional processed prints.

Now everyone seems to be having a go. Public, permanent blinds at wildlife refuges give close views of exciting birds. Digital cameras often have a good zoom lens, and expensive ones work just like single lens reflex cameras and have interchangeable telephoto lenses.

Digiscoping

For decades, astronomers have taken pictures through telescopes—now birders are doing it. With an adapter, you can fasten your camera to a spotting scope and take a picture with it. The quality varies, but can be remarkably good. It is usually called "digiscoping" but there is no reason why the camera has to be digital.

MUST KNOW

Be creative

Try to be imaginative, creative, and artistic if you want to make a mark with your photos. There are plenty of side views of stock-still birds in perfect light perched on sticks: go for action, behavior, or something interesting. Try backlighting for atmosphere. Capture movement. As well as the standard perfect close up, there are increasing outlets for something different; maybe you can exploit them.

Making a start

Now that you're equipped and ready to start birding in earnest, where do you go to see birds? You can head off to some woodland or farmland, a marsh or a lake. However, your own backyard may be the best place to start.

Where to watch birds

Head for water, which always offers much more variety than dry land, even more so in arid areas than elsewhere. You can also see birds that live in habitats beside the water. Rivers are interesting and are often attractive places to visit, but their birdlife is probably less varied than a lowland lake. Lakes in mountains are often deep, cold, and relatively birdless. Reservoirs and artificial lakes can be fine for birds, but this will partly depend on the nature of their edges—concrete

▼ Watery places mean both waterbirds and landbirds can be seen in the same area, almost guaranteeing you a greater variety of species on a single visit.

ones have their moments, but are usually not ideal. Most neighborhoods are within reach of some kind of lake, which can be outstanding for loons, ducks, grebes, gulls, and even waterside birds such as herons and egrets. Reservoirs and sewage lagoons may attract shorebirds and gulls.

Woodland or forest may seem the natural place to see birds, but they can be hard work in summer when the leaves are dense and dark, and also in winter when many birds migrate south or move into gardens or shrubbery. Woods are best for birds in the spring.

▲ Blue jays are popular, but they do provoke differences of opinion. Although they are undoubtedly attractive, they eat some eggs of small birds for a time in the spring, and often chase all the birds away from a feeding station.

Feeding the birds

At home in the backyard, foods and feeders will attract a wide variety of birds. Such great birds as American goldfinches and ruby-throated hummingbirds are attracted by hanging feeders, while bird-houses help attract anything from bluebirds, wrens, and chickadees to screech owls and wood ducks.

Feeding birds has become a multi-million dollar industry. Look in the bird magazines for advertisements and get some catalogs and bird feeding guides—they give excellent advice, while naturally plugging their own products.

Platform feeders

A tray or platform feeder is not essential, but it looks good and does provide a fixed point for watching birds. A simple flat board on a post is best, or a board hung with a chain at each end (to stop tangling) from a snag.

Trays attract birds, but don't provide much protection from the weather or from squirrels or chipmunks. A roof will help with the former (and may also deter larger birds such as jays). Trays need some attention, as their surface soon becomes matted with leftover food and bird excreta; clean them at least every two weeks.

▶ European Starlings are opportunists but are not ideally suited to feed on hard peanuts from a mesh feeder. If you wish to feed them, they may rely on being able to take mashed pieces of peanuts broken up by other birds.

> **MUST KNOW**
>
> ### Hoppers
> These are modified platform feeders, in which the seed is dispensed from a container on to a tray. As the birds eat, gravity replenishes the supply. Hoppers are filled from the top, by removing the roof, which also provides some shelter for both food and birds.

◀ An acorn woodpecker visits a platform feeder in a southwestern yard. Platforms provide great fixed sites for us to watch and photograph our backyard birds.

Hanging feeders

Either hung from trees, or from the edges of the tray, hanging feeders are perfect, as they give birds space and food while allowing them to show off their acrobatic prowess. Feeders can be purchased in two main types:

● The plastic tube with "ports" through which food is dispensed at a controlled rate.

● Mesh baskets or cages, which are made of non-rusting stainless steel or plastic mesh. The basket types are useful for larger nuts and seeds, household scraps, and for suet or fat. The latter are particularly good for woodpeckers and nuthatches, although they also attract chickadees, titmice, and jays.

The tube types are better for fine seed mixes. The finest, such as niger (or "thistle seed"), may

▼ This female ruby-throated hummingbird is visiting a saucer-style feeder filled with sugar solution.

require a special adapted feeder, as this tiny seed is easily blown away and wasted. It seems to work like magic in some backyards, bringing in goldfinches, pine siskins, and redpolls where none has been seen before.

You can also get all manner of seed hoppers, ground hoppers, and caged-in feeders, which supposedly keep out squirrels and sparrowhawks. The ground hoppers help feed species of birds that prefer to be low down, but they keep food tidy, dry, and fresh.

Hummingbird feeders

All you need to feed hummers is a container to hold artificial nectar or sugar solution. There are two main types—bottle/tube feeders and saucer styles—which are available commercially. You can also make your own using a bottle, rubber cork, and the drinking tube from a pet's water bottle. Put something red on it, even just a ribbon, to attract the hummingbirds. Include guards to deter bees and ants. Make sure you wash any hummer feeder frequently.

Other feeders

There are any number of specialist feeders on the market, some of them suitable for just a single species of bird. These can be expensive, so make sure your desired bird does actually occur in your neighborhood before buying one.

Hygiene

It is essential to keep feeders clean. From time to time, use a very mild solution of bleach (barely 10 percent in water) and wash them down, then rinse thoroughly. Put food out as required—don't throw out tons of food and hope more birds will arrive. Wasted food can rot, which is unsightly, potentially unhealthy, and may attract rats. Adjust your supply to the demand.

WATCH OUT!

Cleaning
Use cleaning utensils that you keep solely for this purpose and don't mix them with anything you used elsewhere, as birds can and do carry disease (salmonella is not exceptional). You must be careful to look after yourself as well as your backyard guests.

Which foods?

Be inventive when you feeding birds. You can smear waste fat and cheese into the bark of a tree, for instance, to help woodpeckers, wrens, and nuthatches. Birds need high-fat diets for energy. You can scatter currants, fruit, crumbled pie crust, bread, and cake around the edge of a flower border or a hedge, to feed ground-feeding species like sparrows, towhees, and juncos, which prefer not to come to a platform feeder.

▲ Fresh fruit is often very attractive to backyard birds, especially in the southern U.S. Even so, not many of us will receive visits from the rare green jay.

Water

As well as all this food, water is essential for birds, even in winter. A birdbath is ideal, but you need to keep it clean and topped up; in areas where freezing is commonplace you might have to purchase an all-weather heating element and, indeed, some birdbaths come with these fitted. A birdbath is best if it is shallow at the edges but deeper toward one end, so any birds from chickadee to jay size can get in and bathe or drink. Water can be as much of an attraction to birds as regular food, and just as rare in snowy or dry conditions, so don't forget to provide it.

FOODS TO PROVIDE

- Bird seed mixtures containing flaked corn, sunflower seeds, or peanut granules.
- Millet is good for doves, juncos, and sparrows. Most birds that like millet feed on the ground, so it is not always suitable in a hanging feeder.
- Whole corn is good for jays, doves, and gamebirds such as quail.
- Flaked corn attracts blackbirds and sparrows.
- Black sunflower seeds are excellent year-round food for almost all your favorite species. Also available hulled.
- Safflower seeds are favorites of cardinals, and can apparently be a turnoff to European starlings, grackles, cowbirds, and house sparrows.
- Niger seeds are very small, but have a high oil content and are ideal for goldfinches, pine siskins, redpolls, and indigo buntings.
- Peanuts are rich in fats and popular with chickadees, nuthatches, woodpeckers, cardinals, jays, and some sparrows, including the introduced house sparrow. They are best placed in a feeder with fine mesh.
- Raw suet (the fat surrounding the kidneys of cows and sheep) is great for a good many species, especially woodpeckers and nuthatches.
- Fat balls and food bars are popular with many species.
- Cheese is an alternative fat-supplying food, beloved of robins and wrens.
- Peanut butter is high in fat and protein and can be smeared in bark, or even into hanging pine cones.
- Dried fruits can bring in species such as catbirds, bluebirds, robins, and mockingbirds. Raisins are ideal, especially if soaked in water to soften them first.
- Oatmeal is popular with some species.
- Apples, pears, and other fresh fruit can be cut up.
- Pie crust, cooked or uncooked, is excellent, especially made with real fats.
- Crumbled bread is suitable, but in small quantities as its nutritional value is relatively low. Moisten if very dry; brown is better than white.
- Don't forget your hummers. Make up a four-to-one sugar/water solution and watch the fun!

WATCH OUT!

Foods to avoid
- Wheat and barley mixtures, if you only want to attract smaller birds.
- Milo (sorghum) is ignored by most small birds, but might attract the less desirable species such as European starlings and grackles.
- Split peas, beans, dried rice, or lentils attract only large species.
- Salted or dry-roasted peanuts (avoid at all times; they can be harmful).
- Polyunsaturated fats, low-fat spreads, and low-fat foods—birds need fat.

Nestboxes

Nestboxes, or bird-houses, are quite specialized garden equipment, but a simple wooden box for chickadees, for example, is easy to make. Although you can buy one, you should be careful to purchase only from companies that actually understand the needs of birds. Never, for example, buy a box with a perch under the hole, as it is so easy to do; the perch will simply help predators to get in. All-in-one houses and feeders are to be avoided at all costs.

For most backyard birds, a box which is about 12" square inside is suitable, with at least 6" below the entrance hole. Then it's your

▼ Eastern bluebirds are among the most regular and popular users of artificially provided nesting boxes.

GETTING STARTED

decision as to what diameter you want the hole to be, as different measurements will suit different birds. For example, a diameter of 1.25" is good for chickadees and nuthatches, while 1.5" will suit bluebirds; 2" is good for great crested flycatchers, and 3.25" may attract a screech owl.

As with all matters to do with backyard birds, there is a commercial market to suit all tastes, and you can buy special "homes" for purple martins and other species for a few dollars more.

Make sure you put up your bird-houses long before the breeding season begins, which means February in southern areas and mid to late March in the north. They should be sited carefully, well out of reach of ground predators; indeed, many enthusiasts place their bird-houses on inaccessible poles put up especially for the purpose. Don't forget to put up several boxes for colonial species, such as bluebirds or swallows.

MUST KNOW

Nestboxes
For more details, you can contact a national bird organization or look at a catalog from a reputable birdfood or garden bird equipment supplier—birding and other outdoor magazines usually list plenty of them.

Wildlife landscaping

To a bird, a good backyard will have three things it needs: food, water, and shelter. The food may come from the feeding stations provided by the owner, but a particularly good and lasting way of helping all kinds of wildlife is to put in the right kind of plants. As a general rule, it is good to plant native species, and make sure you select both showy plants, which attract insects, and fruit-producing plants, such as bayberry and dogwoods. Plant native trees, if you can, such as mulberries or oaks, and allow native vines and creepers to grow.

Of course, what you can do depends not only on how much space you have, but also what sort of climate you are living in. But everybody can do something, and this kind of landscaping is worthwhile and often very satisfying. There is always something special about seeing the birds using something that you have put in place.

want to know more?

Take it to the next level...

Go to...
▶ **Backyard birds** page 128
▶ **Cities and urban fringes** page 136
▶ **Forests and woodland** page 152

Other sources
▶ **Your local bird club**
  for local knowledge and expert advice
▶ **Your local library**
  for books on local birdlife
▶ **Internet**
  for information and personal experience
▶ **Gardening books and magazines**
  for plants that attract birds
▶ **Publications**
  visit www.buteobooks.com for bird books

birds

All North American birds can fly (although some other birds, elsewhere in the world, lost the power of flight long ago) but so do insects and bats. All birds lay eggs—but insects, reptiles, fish, and even a few mammals also do this. So what makes birds unique and different? A combination of features, plus a coating of feathers, sets birds apart from other creatures.

Bird anatomy

Birds are akin to reptiles. In fact, some people think that they are modified reptiles, having been derived from small, active dinosaurs, though there is some controversy over this. They have bony skeletons with a backbone of many vertebrae (not unlike a reptile's), strong, slender ribs, a pelvis that supports the hind limbs, forelimbs with digits fused together toward the tips of the wings, a small, lightweight skull, and bones that are light and penetrated by airways which allow great strength but reduce weight for flight.

Designed for flight

A flying bird has a deep breastbone, or sternum, to which are attached strong pectoral muscles (the powerhouse for flight). A bird like a wild turkey or rock dove has enormous muscles attached to the breastbone, giving a deep-chested shape and great acceleration—high speed from a standing start which takes the bird away from predators.

▼ The bald eagle (this is an immature bird) has broad, deeply-fingered wingtips for powerful, stable flight. Here it is seen among some Northern pintails.

Other birds, such as hawks (Buteos) and vultures, have weak breast muscles but wings of a very large surface area. They cannot beat them powerfully or quickly, but they ride air currents and glide superbly well—masters of the air, traveling far almost effortlessly. Between the two extremes are many forms with greater or lesser power in the air.

Beaks, legs, and feet

Birds have jaws which are clothed with tough, bony sheaths to give a strong beak: An upper mandible with little or no movement relative to the skull; and a lower mandible with considerable vertical, but little sideways, motion. Beaks are characteristic of birds but they vary greatly in both their shape and detail.

Birds' legs and feet may be fully feathered or quite bare, hard, and scaly, with more or less arched "nails" in the form of claws. Like beaks, legs and feet are strongly adapted to the way of life that is characteristic of a particular bird.

Parts of a bird

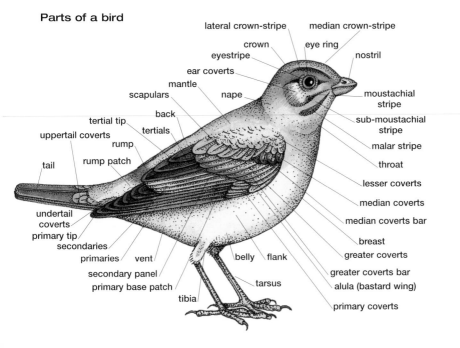

lateral crown-stripe
median crown-stripe
crown
eye ring
eyestripe
nostril
ear coverts
mantle
scapulars
nape
moustachial stripe
back
sub-moustachial stripe
tertial tip
tertials
malar stripe
uppertail coverts
rump
throat
tail
rump patch
lesser coverts
median coverts
median coverts bar
undertail coverts
breast
primary tip
secondaries
greater coverts
primaries
vent
belly
flank
greater coverts bar
secondary panel
alula (bastard wing)
primary base patch
tarsus
primary coverts
tibia

Feathers

A bird's feather is a remarkable structure. It is essentially composed of keratin, the horny substance that forms the basis for human fingernails. It is strong but light in weight, both of which are essential qualities for a bird.

The structure of feathers

Each feather has a more or less central shaft or, in the larger ones, a quill. Large quills have a hollow base and they taper to a solid, narrow tip. On each side is the "vane" or "web", composed of a complex structure of barbs, which grow out at an angle from the shaft, and barbules, which are like tiny hooks that zipper together (a little like Velcro attachments) and keep the barbs together as a strong, flat sheet. If the barbules become disarranged, a bird can simply zipper them together again by running the feather through its bill, otherwise known as preening.

The smaller feathers are loose with fewer interconnecting barbules. They form the soft down that insulates the bird beneath its covering of stronger "contour" feathers, so called because they help shape the body into the characteristic form of each species.

> **MUST KNOW**
>
> **Primary feathers**
> The wingtip feathers, called the primary feathers, are stiff and strong, but, in a fast, deep wingbeat, their tips will twist under pressure and act like miniature propellers, forcing the bird forward as the wing is pushed down.

▼ Feathers add color and pattern to a bird, as well as essential insulation and weatherproofing.

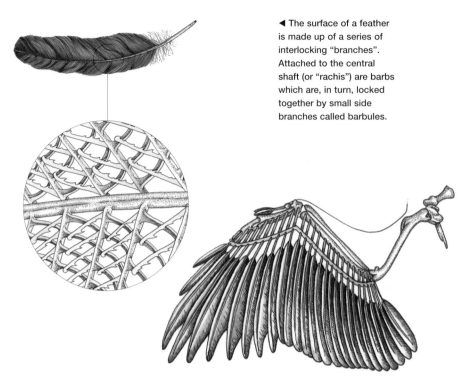

◄ The surface of a feather is made up of a series of interlocking "branches". Attached to the central shaft (or "rachis") are barbs which are, in turn, locked together by small side branches called barbules.

The larger feathers on the wing and the tail are the "flight feathers". They have a much stiffer shaft and strong vanes that are wider on one side than the other, to give an aerodynamic shape which helps the bird to fly.

▲ A bird's wing with all the smaller feathers removed. You can see that the bones are similar to those in a human arm.

Molting and function

Feathers grow from "germs" within the skin (the familiar "goose-bumps" on a plucked fowl) and can be shed and replaced once or twice each year, in a process called molt. In this way, they maintain a well-conditioned, sleek plumage that covers the body of a bird, growing from well-defined tracts over the skin.

Feathers provide warmth and insulation, waterproofing, color, and adornment, both in terms of pattern and shape. Without feathers, birds would have little or none of their uniquely colorful and dramatic character.

Flight

Birds are remarkable, not least for their ability to fly. They have an amazing ability for instant directional changes, acceleration, and deceleration, and many migratory birds that fly at night navigate by the stars.

The mechanics of flight

Flight is achieved by several means, often in combination. Pure power, from the large muscles in the breast, pulls the wings downward and creates lift, by pressing the surface of the wings against the air. This takes a huge amount of energy, and, for larger birds, such powered flight may be short-lived. However, it can be extended by a glide—using the surface of the wing as an aerofoil to maintain height as the bird sails forward through the air. For example, a ring-necked pheasant, disturbed from the ground, rises with a great clatter of wings and flies off at great speed but, within seconds, has to glide on outstretched wings before landing at a run and dashing off into cover. It simply cannot maintain this high-speed escape for long.

▲ This gannet is about to land, with its legs dangling, tail slightly spread, head up and wings markedly angled. All are designed to reduce speed and to add stability

Achieving lift

The upper surface of the bird's wing is convex, whereas the lower surface is flat or slightly concave, so air rushing over the top of the wing has further to travel than air beneath it. Air hitting the leading edge of the wing is split—half going above, half going below—to reach the back of the wing at the same time.

To avoid creating a vacuum, the air above the wing must move faster. The pressure on the upper surface of the wing is reduced; the higher pressure below tends to push the bird upward. This is exactly the same principle as that used in the design of an aircraft's wing.

Simple pressure against the air also pushes the bird higher, so long as it can move forward and angle its wings slightly upward. Forward motion can be gained by, for example, jumping from a ledge, as a murre does when setting out to sea. But the bird might simply fly head to wind, using the movement of the wind currents to create lift against its wing surfaces.

Air currents

Seabirds use complex air currents very low over the waves, which take them hundreds of miles over the ocean with very little effort. Their long, narrow wings are perfect for such long-distance gliding, but they create so much force against the air beneath that they are not suited for quick wingbeats in powered flight.

▼ The long, narrow wings of this Arctic tern are made for long-distance flying and extra maneuverability when hovering and diving for fish. The tail-streamers help it to "steer" in its dive.

Soaring on thermals

Big soaring birds, such as pelicans and turkey
vultures, seek out rising pockets of air, called
thermals, which "bubble" up over warm hillsides,
and even roads and cities, and circle within
them to gain a great height. Then they head to
wherever they want to go and simply glide away,
losing height very slowly to give forward motion
and lift, as they simply use gravity to power their
movements, with no effort at all. In soaring mode,
they spread their long, broad wings to the
utmost, and their wingtip feathers are parted like
"fingers" to gain the greatest possible lift. In the
downward glide, the wings are more angled with
the feathers closed together to reduce drag.

Overcoming drag

Small birds, such as warblers and sparrows, are
so stout-bodied relative to their overall size that
they have to overcome problems with drag—the

▲ The broad, powerful
wings of a turkey vulture
help it to gain height. When
the bird is in a current of
rising air, their great spread
gives enormous lift and it
can fly on with very little
expenditure of energy.

friction of the air against their bodies, which slows them down. They do this by using fast bursts of wingbeats to thrust themselves forward and upward, then rest for a moment with their wings closed, diving forward and downward, until the next burst of beats. This gives them a characteristic swooping flight pattern.

Landing

When a bird comes in to land, it raises its head and body upward and backward, opens the alula as an airbrake, thrusts forward its feet, angles its wings, and spreads its tail, using as much surface area as it can to slow down. By delicately adjusting its wings, tail, and feet it makes a perfect touchdown, whether on ground, water, or a slender perch.

With small birds, such as chickadees landing on a nut basket, the action is so fast that we can hardly see it. To do this, a bird needs excellent eyesight and superb judgment; these must be instinctive, not calculated, in exactly the same way that we might reach up and catch a tennis ball. We could not "calculate" the precise speed and angle of both the ball and hand but just "catch" it without thinking. No doubt a bird flies and settles in just the same way, performing complex maneuvers without having to think about what it is doing.

◀ Just prior to landing, this snow goose can be seen to lower its body and spread its tail, causing it to slow down.

Life cycle

Birds lay eggs and incubate them externally, in a nest, unlike mammals whose fertilized eggs grow internally inside a uterus. The nest is used solely to hold the eggs during incubation and, in many species, the chicks while they grow their first feathers. A nest is not a "house" which is used all year round, although some nest holes and old nests may be used in winter as roost sites overnight, to keep a bird warm and sheltered.

Incubation

An egg has a yolk, white, and airspace inside a fine membrane, within a calcium shell. It is "incubated" (kept at a constant temperature while the embryo develops inside). The warmth comes from a bare patch of skin on the bird, called a "brood patch," which is full of swollen blood vessels.

Most birds lay more than one egg, one a day over several days, and, when they have finished, incubate them together (as a "clutch"). Some species, such as owls, incubate from the day the first egg is laid. As each egg hatches out after about the same number of days, the chicks hatch out at intervals and the first-hatched are considerably larger than the last-hatched, at least for the first days until all are fully grown.

MUST KNOW

Laying times
Most birds lay their eggs in spring, the time depending upon latitude. A species that starts in March in the Southern States may be delayed until May in the North. Each species has its specific start times and some are earlier than others. How long eggs take to hatch depends on their size; as little as 10 days for very small birds but 50 or more for larger ones.

◀ Here a parasitic jaeger is about to settle on its camouflaged eggs. It will turn them at intervals to prevent the membranes around the embryo becoming stuck to the inside of the eggshell.

Rearing the young

Many species, like robins and mourning doves, lay several clutches during the summer: They are multi-brooded. Robins feed their young on the sort of bugs which are never superabundant but are usually available for a relatively long period of time. Mourning doves only produce two eggs per clutch; the adults feed the young on "milk" that they manufacture in their crops.

A single clutch

Other birds, as varied as ducks, hawks, owls, and most chickadees, lay only one clutch per year, literally putting all their eggs in one basket: They are single-brooded. In the case of larger birds, such as eagles and other raptors, this is because the process of hatching eggs and rearing young takes so long that only one family can be raised per season (the California condor only lays one clutch every two years). Chickadees, however, time their breeding in the spring to coincide with the short-term abundance of foods like caterpillars.

Development of chicks

Once hatched, the chicks may be naked and blind at first and remain in the nest until they are well feathered and able to fly (as with songbirds and raptors) or they may leave the nest within hours, clothed in down and already able to walk, swim, and feed themselves (as with gamebirds, wildfowl, and shorebirds).

Small birds, like warblers and wrens, are full grown when they leave the nest and independent within a week or 10 days, while big ones, such as geese, may stay with their parents through their first winter of life, to be driven away next spring when they are almost a year old. Birds with specialist "trades," like hunting owls and hawks, may need a longer dependence on their parents than most as they learn how to feed themselves.

▲ This female yellow warbler is feeding its chicks. The biggest and fittest get fed first, as it makes no sense wasting good food on sickly chicks that might die. If there is sufficient food, they will be fed later, and still survive.

Breeding systems

There are many different breeding systems used by birds. In some, such as the one employed by the mallard and other ducks, the male mates with the female but takes no part in nest building, incubating the eggs, or looking after chicks. The same applies to some gamebird species, notably grouse. Males of these species may copulate with several different females in a season. Other birds, such as wood thrushes, share family duties and may even split the brood between them after they leave the nest, when they are able to fly but still dependent on their parents for food.

In many species, the female plays the greater part in incubation while the male finds food for the female as she tends the eggs and the growing family afterwards. Some are bigamous, others monogamous, but even in "socially monogamous" species, like the barn swallow and bluebirds, females take every opportunity to mate with other males. Many of their young are fathered by males other than their regular mates.

▼ These male ring-necked pheasants fight fiercely to win the attentions of a female. It is the female bird, for all her duller colors, that has the final choice of mate.

A few species have reversed roles, in which the female lays eggs for the male to incubate, then leaves the area, so the male also has to look after the growing family—the spotted sandpiper is an example. The phalaropes have taken role reversal still further; the males incubate the eggs and look after the young, and have duller plumage than the females, having surrendered the usual male prerogative of initiating courtship display.

Young of some species may help parents to look after subsequent broods. They include common moorhens, purple gallinules, Florida scrub jays, and red-cockaded woodpeckers. Several unrelated adult Smith's longspurs may find themselves feeding the same young in the same nest because of a system of sharing mates.

A few birds are "brood parasites," laying eggs in other birds' nests rather than building their own and looking after their own young. Cowbirds are notorious for this and have been known to parasitize 200 or more different species. Their chicks often out-compete the young of the host, causing the latter to starve; thus cowbirds can adversely affect the populations of their favored hosts in any particular location.

▲ A common moorhen with its chick. Young moorhens reared in the spring may help their parents to feed small chicks from broods reared later in the summer.

MUST KNOW

Incubation
Most birds do not begin to incubate their eggs until the full clutch is laid, so that all hatch out more or less together, and all the young are of the same size and age from the start. Young in the nest together are referred to as a "brood."

What is a species?

A species is not a "breed." "Breeds" are usually variations of an animal or plant which are produced by centuries of selective breeding; for instance, Border Collies and Bull Terriers, and Rambouillets and Suffolks are breeds of dog and sheep respectively. The species are the dog and the sheep.

Bird species

Species arise naturally, but defining what they are exactly is not always easy. The concept that has been used over many years is that "species are groups of interbreeding natural populations that are reproductively isolated from other such groups." This works well when two different kinds of birds live in the same area. For example, downy and hairy woodpeckers are clearly distinct kinds. Their breeding ranges overlap, but they don't mate with one another and are "reproductively isolated." They are kept separate by many things:

- Their genetic make-up
- Their appearance

◀ We may find it difficult to tell a hairy woodpecker (as here) from a downy woodpecker, but the birds don't, and it stops them interbreeding with one another.

- Their vocalizations
- The details of their behavior.

If they did ever interbreed ("crossbreed") to produce hybrid young, in some cases the two kinds would merge into one.

Subject to interpretation

When similar birds live in separate areas, it can be difficult to decide whether they are different species. Western and eastern populations of the scrub jay were previously considered one species, but they have since been split into separate ones, with another on islands off the California coast. When two populations live far apart we don't have any proof whether or not they will interbreed should they meet, so the decision as to what is a species becomes a matter of interpretation—a subjective judgment.

Bullock's and Baltimore orioles are among a number of species that differ from east to west. The Baltimore oriole is the eastern version, with a completely black head in the male, whereas Bullock's oriole, the western version, has only a black throat, crown, and eyestripe, but also has much more white in the wing. The birds meet in several zones of overlap and produce fertile offspring when they hybridize.

The two have been considered as "races" or "subspecies" for some time under the bland umbrella name of "Northern oriole," but recently they have been split again and treated by scientists as two separate species.

Something prevents the distinctions between them disappearing; there must be something beneficial about being one or the other that has maintained the difference all this time—this is good evidence that they really are separate species. Recent genetic studies, indeed, have shown that they are not as closely related as was originally perceived.

▲ The black head of this male oriole identifies it as the Baltimore oriole, the species found in the east.

▲ Reddish egrets occur in two color morphs, one gray and reddish, as here, and one that is pure white. Even so, they are one and the same species. Such are the complications of bird speciation.

▲ Parasitic jaegers are seen in several types. This one is a "pale morph" bird, but some are dark brown all over.

MUST KNOW

Polymorphic
There are polymorphic species with more than one variety, which can pair together and produce young of either type. The parasitic jaeger comes in both dark and pale forms, but these behave alike. They can and do interbreed all the time.

A new definition?

There is a growing trend toward a new concept of species—the phylogenetic species concept—which says that different geographic forms of the same basic "kind" of bird should be treated as distinct species. This is because these forms have evolved separately and have unique evolutionary histories. There is no need to worry about whether they might interbreed. If they don't, they can be treated as full species. This would create many more species than we have become accustomed to.

Biological species concept

The traditional theory is the biological species concept, which is based on the idea that if genes can be shared between groups (because they can interbreed and produce healthy, fertile offspring), then these groups can and do influence each other genetically and are the same species.

However, the newer, phylogenetic species concept assumes that we can tell which groups are affecting each other genetically. Thus if the members of a group share a characteristic that is not found in other groups, such as the white-fronted geese that are found in Greenland (dark plumaged, orange-billed) and the North American tundra (smaller and paler-billed), then they are separate, and they are clearly not spreading their features to the others. So they are separate species.

▼ The Greenland white-fronted goose is a tricky problem—is it a different race or is it a separate species altogether from the similar continental-breeding white-fronted goose?

▶ Varieties and variations

There are variations of birds that we can see, which are neither species nor subspecies. These differences are trivial and superficial, such as patches of white on a mildly abnormal American crow, or the presence or absence of a white neck collar on a male ring-necked pheasant. This may be confusing initially.

How varieties arise

Varieties arise from centuries of domestication and selective breeding. Domestic ducks illustrate this well. They come from two kinds: The mallard (common in North America) and the muscovy duck (a South American bird). Mallards gave rise to Pekin ducks (white with orange bills) and other types that can be all black-brown, brown with a white breast, or a dull fawn color with a hint of a darker green head. Sometimes these barnyard ducks go wild and mix with wild mallards. They are still the same species and can interbreed, but they don't interbreed with, for example, wild pintails or wigeons. You may see many variations as a result on a local lake.

▼ Mallards are true wild ducks but they are easily tamed and domesticated. Most barnyard varieties come from this species or from the South American muscovy duck.

Unusual wild birds

Some genuinely wild birds look unusual. If they have too little pigment, which is a minor genetic fault, they may be extremely pale. For instance, you may have seen a sandy-brown house sparrow or starling. These are "leucistic" birds. With no pigment at all they become white (albinistic). With an excess of pigment (more rarely seen) they are very dark and are called "melanistic." There are rare variations with too much red (erythristic) or yellow (xanthocroistic) but you are unlikely to see these.

Irregular patterns

You will often see individuals that are "part albino" or "part leucistic," such as crows with whitish wingbars (probably a result of poor nutrition), cardinals with white patches, and house sparrows with white on the wings and tail. These patterns are irregular but often symmetrical. They may miss a generation but crop up again in later ones, rather like red hair and freckles in a human family.

▲ This albinistic ring-necked pheasant certainly stands out from the rest of its kind.

> **MUST KNOW**
>
> **Feathers**
> Some domestic bird variations have odd feathers: Ducks with curly tufts on their heads and rock doves with strange plumes around their feet. These are obviously "strange" and often too tame to confuse with some wild migrant out of its normal range.

▶ Rarities

Rare birds come in three kinds: Birds that are very scarce, even in areas where they are regularly seen; birds that have migrated too far in one direction, such as north in spring; and birds that have gone hundreds of miles off course and end up in North America when they should be in, say, Europe or Asia.

Examples of rarities

Long-eared owls are a good example of a bird that is widespread, but often very difficult to find. Lesser prairie chickens, on the other hand, are found only on natural arid prairies, a much reduced and fragmented habitat, so they too are hard to find.

Birds that migrate off course may be storm-driven waifs, or may be so far off course that we can only assume that their internal navigation systems have somehow gone altogether wrong.

> **WATCH OUT!**
>
> **Be wary**
> Not all potential rarities turn out as exciting as you might hope. They are often escapees from zoos and ornamental wildfowl collections. These are not genuine strays from far-off regions; they have strayed from an insecure aviary or a park lake.

◀ Golden eagles have huge ranges over which they hunt, and in most parts of North America they can be difficult to see. That does not, however, necessarily class them as rarities.

Listers

Not so long ago, birders had to find rarities for themselves, but it is now possible, via telephone and internet rare bird alerts, to be directed to new finds as soon as they arrive.

Why are people so attracted to rare birds? A very obvious answer is that most birders enjoy making lists of birds they've seen, and the longer the list the better. After a few years' birding, most beginners have seen a high proportion of their local species and need to add only the rarer ones. However, you are unlikely to come across rare birds all by yourself—you need the relevant bird information network to help you.

A few bird lovers are critical of listers, and it's true that some people can become obsessive in their quest for "lifers," and travel the length and breadth of the continent to seek out an obscure bird with distinctive spots found by someone else. But really, it is only a matter of degree as to what sort of lister you are. Most of us go birding just to enjoy the birds, but that feeling of seeing something new is certainly a special one.

▲ Most birders are simply watchers of birds. But true listers are different. They travel long distances to see a specific bird, which is the sole object of the exercise.

Migration

This is the regular, seasonal movement of whole populations of birds across the surface of the earth. Some stay in the same place all year, and may change their diet with the seasons, eating insects in summer, for example, and worms, fruit, or seeds in winter. Others eat insects all year but must move from place to place to find them—they migrate. Many birds migrate to exploit an abundance of food available only at certain times.

Heading north

The Arctic is fearsomely cold and dark from fall to spring, but in the summer, it has twenty-four hours of daylight each day for a short period and, when the shallow soils and abundant pools thaw, insects and their larvae are superabundant and small mammals that hibernate all winter are active again. No birds can live there for many months, but during the summer there is a fabulous food supply and huge numbers move north to exploit it. They include shorebirds, ducks, geese, gulls, terns, jaegers, and birds of prey.

▼ Migrating birds are often inconspicuous, traveling at night, but sometimes flocks of shorebirds, blackbirds, or geese show us that birds are on the move in numbers.

Shorebirds

Shorebirds heading to the Arctic in spring linger in their winter quarters until May—they have no need to go north until the snow and ice have melted. Then they rush north to find the best breeding territories, competing with fellow travelers as soon as they arrive.

Many are paired already, ready to nest as soon as they arrive on the tundra. To exploit the brief summer to the full, some female shorebirds lay several clutches of eggs in quick succession and allot the job of incubating each one to a different male. There is no time for a conventional pair to rear several broods in succession, as by early July they must start to head south. They can be seen in the "winter" quarters for ten or eleven months of the year.

▲ The red knot breeds as far north as any shorebird in the world.

MUST KNOW

Arctic birds
Many change their habitat and diet when they migrate south. From breeding beside freshwater tundra pools and subsisting on insects, many become coastal, feeding on mollusks and crustaceans.

Wildfowl

These also pair up in winter and dash north, ready to breed as soon as conditions are right. Male ducks tend to follow their mates "home," rather than the females returning to where the male was born. This need for early pairing is why ducks are at their best, in full breeding colors, from late fall onwards, and why they are so often seen in courtship display in their wintering areas.

Duck pairs usually split up early; males leave the females in sole charge of the family before the eggs hatch. They vacate the breeding areas and gather together in favorable areas to molt; the females and young join a few weeks later. Only then do ducks start migrating.

Geese and swans behave differently to ducks. These birds form lifelong pair bonds, and the whole family, adults and young, migrates as a unit after the breeding season.

▼ A distinctive "V" of geese at sunset is a very beautiful and evocative sight in many areas near large lakes or coastal marshes.

Heading south

To the south of the Arctic conditions are not so severe, but across much of temperate North America most insect-eaters are still excluded in winter and must go south to survive, often to the Caribbean or Central and South America. In spring, however, there is a rush northward as new sources become available and millions of wood warblers, thrushes, swallows, flycatchers, vireos, tanagers, and buntings are on the move, as well as many others. The day length and temperature control their movements.

Summer visitors and migrants

Almost throughout North America the resident birds can be joined, for several months in the spring and fall, not just by the summer visitors arriving to breed, but also by "passage migrants" in transit north or south. This fabulous mix of different birds makes the spring and fall periods an exciting time for the birder, as there is so much to see, so many birds migrating—each day may bring new arrivals and unexpected finds.

▲ Swallows gather on wires before migrating to Africa in the fall. They provide us with a classic symbol of the advancing seasons.

Small birds

These may migrate anything from 500 to 5,000 miles, putting on weight under the control of special hormones. Our many species of wood warblers have various migration strategies and routes. The pine warbler, for example, may not migrate at all, whereas the blackpoll warbler, breeding mainly in the northern taiga belt, may travel as far south as Brazil for the winter. Several warblers spend the nonbreeding season in the Southern States, especially along the Gulf Coast and Florida, while others go further, to Mexico, taking an overland route; some fly across the Gulf itself to northern South America.

Even closely related species may show different migratory programs: The black-throated blue warbler, for example, migrates down through Florida and the Caribbean, while the bay-breasted warbler crosses over the Gulf to Yucatan, and Townsend's warbler migrates overland through the valleys of the southwest to get to Mexico and Central America. Those species with longer journeys may double their body weight prior to migration, since long crossings over inhospitable territory require a high level of fat fuel. Such crossings may require 20 or 30 hours of nonstop flying.

Hummingbirds

Several hummers occur in North America only in summer and most of these take an overland route on migration. But the irrepressible ruby-throated eschews such comforts, completing its fall journey, or beginning its spring journey, with a crossing of the Gulf of Mexico to and from the Yucatan Peninsula. This involves a nonstop flight of about 500 miles, which the birds carry out overnight, usually at the same times as clouds of other small birds. In order to fuel this almost miraculous undertaking, rubythroats almost

▲ The yellow-rumped warbler is the most prevalent migrating warbler across the United States.

> **MUST KNOW**
>
> ### Adverse conditions
>
> Most migration takes place at night, when birds can see the stars in a clear sky. We may view few birds on the ground in such conditions. When we see large numbers of warblers, vireos, thrushes, and flycatchers around us, however, it is a sign that the weather caught them out overnight and they were forced down by fog, rain, or strong winds. To us, this is a "fallout"; for the birds, it means difficult conditions.

double their body mass, from three to five grams, in the few days prior to setting off.

Hawks

Among the longest migratory journeys undertaken by any North America bird is that of a raptor, the Swainson's hawk. This bird flies from the Prairies (and there is an outpost in Alaska) to the pampas of Argentina for the winter, a journey of up to 7,500 miles. The birds travel by day, and for a good reason; they use uprisings of air, known as thermals, to power their progress, gliding from one thermal to the other, moving ever southward. This enables them to use little in the way of energy.

It does have its problems, though. Thermals only form in dry, warm weather, and they don't form at all over water. So Swainson's hawks, and many other migrant raptors, must avoid sea crossings at all costs, and this can concentrate them in enormous numbers at land bridges, such as Panama, and at raptor watchpoints, such as Cape May in New Jersey. Migrating raptors also follow mountain ranges on their journeys, and this concentrates them along certain valleys or ridges. Birders often gather to watch their progress in hotspots, such as Hawk Mountain in Pennsylania.

▲ At least some individual ruby-throated hummingbirds fly across the Gulf of Mexico on their migration.

▲ The Swainson's hawk probably has the longest migratory journey of any raptor in the world.

Traditional routes

While a young snow goose or sandhill crane will
follow its parents on their long journeys and learn
traditional routes and stopping places that have
been used for thousands of years, the young of
most other birds, from swallows to hummingbirds,
will fly south alone, with no such assistance. Yet
shorebirds like red knots or American golden
plovers fly from the Arctic to the southern parts
of South America in epic journeys, quite unaided.

Returning to the same place

Barn swallows that nest in your backyard will
return to the same place the following year.
Blackburnian warblers will sing from the same
tree as the previous spring and, remarkably, will
use the same patch of forest in Central or South
America during the winter, too. Mourning doves
will return within yards of their previous nest-site
in the spring, regardless of the length of their
migration in the meantime. And many female

▼ Snow geese follow
traditional routes on their
migration across North
America, passed down from
generation to generation.

ducks will return to the same patch of tundra where they themselves were born the previous year, having wintered far to the south, and they will bring a newly-found mate with them. The ability of so many birds to home in on familiar territory from afar is truly remarkable.

Numbered rings

Most of what we know about such amazing feats has been discovered through decades of banding live birds with numbered rings. The birds are released unharmed; if they are later caught again, or found dead, the details on the ring can help us to trace their movements. If you find a banded bird, you should return the ring to the address stamped upon it.

How do they do it?

We know many of the mechanisms that birds use, but migration remains a magical process. Birds must have a very accurate internal clock and calendar. Young birds learn the star patterns overhead and the position of the sun, but these are of no use unless they can be related to the time of day, the season, and the position on the earth's surface from which they are observed. Landbirds learn the contours of the landscapes around them, probably in remarkable detail, so they can home in on their nesting areas once they are in the general vicinity, but seabirds, flying a meter or two above the waves, have no such visible clues.

Some birds have special secretions in their brains, even inside their eyes, that detect the earth's magnetic field, to an extremely high degree of sensitivity. They can see polarized light and therefore can use the position of the sun even on overcast days. In several ways, they are able to orientate themselves and pinpoint their position on the earth's surface.

want to know more?

Take it to the next level...

Go to...
▶ **Identifying birds** page 72
▶ **Habitats for birds** page 116
▶ **Your local area** page 184

Other sources
▶ **Catalogs**
   for buying bird foods and feeders
▶ **Videos and DVDs**
   for more information on birds
▶ **Fieldguides**
   for identifying unfamiliar species
▶ **Internet**
   for information on migration
▶ **Publications**
   visit www.buteobooks.com for bird books

identifying

birds

Identification will come with practice. Some birds are easy to see and relatively simple to identify, whereas others are unique in their appearance but harder to spot. However, many birds look more or less like other species and it may be difficult to get a positive identification. You will need to study them carefully and get good views to be sure of what they are.

Telling birds apart

Like anything else, bird recognition becomes easier with practice, and it takes time to become an expert. No-one expects to learn how to play a piano or become a top-grade football player over a weekend, but many people seem to think that identifying birds can be learned while on vacation or over a few weekends. To be really expert may take years, but these will be years of great pleasure.

The basics of identification

We are all always in the process of learning and developing our hobby. You will soon progress far beyond "identifying" the common birds—you will just "recognize" them (as you already will with blue jays) as you do members of your family, or your favorite type of car; you don't need to check a series of "fieldmarks" each time.

However, even backyard birds may be difficult to identify at first: They tend to fly away against the sky, or sit like tiny dark spots at the top of a tree, or disappear into some foliage and not fly out. Don't worry if this happens; identification will seem difficult and confusing at first but it rapidly becomes easier.

▼ "Bluebird" sounds easy, but it's often difficult to discern more than a wash of powdery blue on the female mountain bluebird.

A good fieldguide (see page 24) is helpful, but a knowledgeable friend is a bonus. You can sit and work things out for yourself, however, and this is the best and most satisfying way. All of us start off by trying to match what we have seen with the pictures in a book, but look at the maps, the habitat details and the time of year when it is in your area (if it visits at all). Then try to consider other possibilities, such as closely similar species that have to be ruled out.

▲ The dark-eyed junco is made up of five geographic races that are difficult to tell apart because of their similar songs and habits. Birders will find it easiest to identify the different species through their color and their range.

Don't jump to conclusions

Go through all the possibilities before deciding on a bird's identity. It's easy to flick through a book until you come to a picture that looks something like the bird you've seen, and to think it must have been that. But this could be unlikely; maybe the bird you saw was in New York and the one in the book is only found in the Midwest. There are many clues buried away in a good fieldguide.

All of us start off by trying to match what we have seen with the pictures in a book, but look at the maps, the habitat details, and the time of year when it is in your area (if it visits at all). Then try to consider other possibilities, such as closely similar species that have to be ruled out.

MUST KNOW

Basic checklist

If you think that you have found the bird you have seen in a book, check the following points:
- Is it found in the area where you saw it?
- Does it live in that habitat?
- Is it there at that time of year?

These are all basic things to check. Many birds are found in temperate North America only in spring, summer, and fall, but they disappear in wintertime. If a bird is usually found in a forest, you are unlikely to see it on an open field. If it is a bird of the marshes, then it is inlikely that it will find its way to your backyard birdfeeders.

▶ The black-capped chickadee is usually slightly larger than the Carolina, and it has a larger pale bar on its closed wing.

▼ Few species look like the distinctive swallow-tailed kite, but with other birds, you may have to look at features and behavioral cues to distinguish from similar species.

Species and families

You will notice that many groups of birds can be grouped into similar species. These are usually obvious families such as gulls, woodpeckers, warblers, and ducks. Learn more about these families and why and how they differ from others, especially what makes birds of one family similar to each other but not like the rest. For example, ducks swim and have webbed feet, but raptors have sharp claws and hooked beaks.

Other differences are more subtle: Chickadees are small, chunky, active, short-billed, stubby-footed birds that bounce about in foliage and dart from tree to tree. Warblers are also small, but are sleeker, less squat, often with longer, thinner bills, and less feverish actions as they slip through trees, bushes, or waterside plants. Flycatchers are drabber in plumage and they have broad-based, flattened bills. Most sit still on perches awaiting insects to appear in the air near them and then darting out to catch them.

▲ Hardly anyone would guess that the roadrunner is actually a member of the cuckoo family.

◄ Some species of birds are instantly recognizable—this is a scissor-tailed flycatcher.

▶ The ferruginous hawk is in a group of hawks known as the "Buteos." These are medium-large birds with short tails but long, broad wings. Other hawks have quite different features, and the difference is made clear by their scientific names.

Scientific names

Families are not always obvious from their English names: Thus, a flicker is a woodpecker, a redpoll is a finch, and a waterthrush is not a thrush but a member of the warbler family. What will help you understand more about their relationships are the birds' scientific names—two-word names in italic print often written after their English name.

The first word shows the bird's genus, so the mallard, teals, gadwall, and shoveler, for example, are all ducks in the genus *Anas*, while the gulls are *Larus*, the cormorants are *Phalacrocorax,* and most thrashers are in the genus *Toxostoma*.

They help you split larger groups into smaller ones. For instance, diurnal raptors come in various types, including "Buteos" (hawks with long, broad wings and short tails, usually seen soaring in the sky), "Accipiters" (mainly smaller hawks with relatively short, blunt-ended wings and long tails, usually found in woods), and falcons (compact, with relatively long tails but with very sharp, pointed wings, usually found in open places). These divisions are so useful that birders will often call a bird by its generic group name before its species can be determined.

MUST KNOW

Elimination

The information in this book will help you to get things sorted out and, by elimination, you will get new birds down to one or two possible families, then into smaller groups, perhaps into just two or three possibilities. When you go into details, such as size and shape, you should be able to pinpoint what you are seeing.

Size

What size is the bird, approximately? It is hard to compare a bird with something familiar, such as a drink can, an apple, or a size 10 shoe, because things are never quite the same shape. An impression of "size" is usually more to do with bulk, which is better expressed by weight than the length from beak to tail (what the books tell you). If you can, compare a strange bird with something nearby, or judge it against your mental impressions of common ones, such as a house finch, cardinal, American robin, mourning dove, mallard, or Canada goose.

Shape

What about a bird's shape? Try to compare it with something you know. Is it pigeon-like except for longer legs, for example, or is it roughly like a white-crowned sparrow, except for a thinner bill?

If you can, note down the details, especially bill shape, leg length, and the shape and length of the tail. Some birds have very distinctive shapes, such as the long neck of a swan, the crest of a cedar waxwing, or the round body and long tail of a gnatcatcher, but many others are not so distinctive. It might be a thick, thin, straight, or curved bill that gives a crucial clue.

▲ Birding is never easy: Even the distinctive shape of this cedar waxwing can be masked behind foliage.

▼ This is one bird you could identify by its shape alone: The long-billed curlew.

Colors and patterns

When you are out birding and you see an unfamiliar bird, you should try to get a good idea of its basic color and pattern. Always jot down some notes or do a quick sketch in your notebook to describe what you see.

Distinctive markings

If you spot a bird that you cannot identify, you must ask yourself some questions. What is the basic body color? Is it different above and below, or is it roughly the same? Is it dark or pale?

Look for a pattern that stands out. What catches your eye? Does the bird have a stripe over or through its eyes? Stripes over the eye (superciliary or eyebrow stripes) are usually pale; stripes through the eye (eyestripes) are often dark. Are there marks on the wings—if so, when closed or open in flight? Birds like flycatchers can often be identified by the nature of the bars on their wing; some ducks and many shorebirds have long pale stripes along the open wing.

Look at the bill: What is its shape? Look at the tail, especially in flight when it may show patches of color at the base or on either side, or stripes of white along each edge. Once you know more about groups of birds, you will remember what to look at most closely for identification purposes.

▲ The black breast-streaks, white supercilium, and gray cap are all good "field marks" for identifying this magnolia warbler.

> **MUST KNOW**
>
> ### Scientific names
>
> Good identification guides will feature birds' scientific names; these are always in italics and consist of two words. The first word helps show which birds are closely related, such as the song sparrow and the swamp sparrow (both *Melospiza*), or the field sparrow and American tree sparrow (both *Spizella*). Although they are all sparrows, the *Melospiza* pair are much more closely related to each other than any *Spizella* sparrow in shape, pattern, flight action, behavior, and call notes.

Shorebirds

Willets, yellowlegs, oystercatchers, and turnstones have bill and leg colors in different combinations, and patterns on their wings and rumps. But if you think you are looking at a long-billed curlew or a whimbrel, the leg and wing colors will not help you—you must look at the bill length and the head patterns.

Warblers

Warblers are easy enough to identify in spring, with their bright colors and patterns. But in the fall many become much less showy, and then the observer must look for such things as eyerings, wingbars, tail-spots, and breast-streaks.

Sparrows

North America is home to a bewildering variety of sparrows, which at first sight all look the same. But look at their head and bill features. Field, black-chinned, and Harris's sparrows all have distinctive small pink bills, while the sage, black-throated, lark, and golden-crowned sparrows can all be recognized at a glance by their unique head patterns.

▼ The unique head pattern of the black-throated sparrow, as shown here, readily separates it from its host of close relatives.

Changing feathers

The colors of feathers are created by pigments or, in some cases, such as the throat patches of hummingbirds, by reflections of light (like those on a CD or from oil on water). Once a feather has grown, its basic color and pattern are fixed, but it can still change in various ways.

▲ There is little yearly variation in the plumage of a winter wren, a bird that is easily identified by its characteristically upright tail and round shape.

Patterns and colors

These may vary within a species according to age, season, and sex. Some, such as the house wren and American crow, have little variation and look the same at any time. Others, such as large gulls, may take several years to become fully adult and will have a series of intermediate plumages, as well as summer and winter variations for each. Most small birds, however, have a recognizable juvenile plumage which soon changes into the adult pattern. Some birds, such as the yellow-throated or worm-eating warbler, have the same colors whether they are male or female, whereas male and female black-throated blue warblers, for example, are very different.

Constant colors

It is astonishing how remarkably alike most individuals of any one species, age, or sex are, even across the whole of the North American continent. Mourning doves and Eastern kingbirds are good examples of this insofar as the individuals look much alike wherever you go (although they have separate adult and juvenile plumages). In the same way, millions of ring-billed gulls have precisely the same shade of gray on their backs and wings, and the bottle-green on a mallard's head is just the same on the heads of every member of the wild population north of Mexico.

On the other hand, a number of North American species have populations that vary strongly in color from place to place, especially from east to west. Yellow-rumped warblers on the west side of the United States, for example, have yellow throats, while those in the east have white throats, enough for them to have originally been formerly described as separate species, the Audubon's and myrtle warblers respectively. Other species that are highly variable from one location to another include the fox sparrow and the dark-eyed junco.

Constant patterns

Their patterns, too, are surprisingly alike, right down to the finest detail. For example, three very similar species, the Connecticut, mourning, and MacGillivray's warblers, are best told apart by the extent of white on their eyering.

More basic patterns are usually relatively constant. For example, red-breasted nuthatches always have a bold black stripe through the eye, while white-breasted nuthatches, by contrast, have a plain white face. American redstarts always have a bright orange or yellow base to the tail, and white-winged scoters are always easily distinguished from black scoters by their white panel on the trailing edge of the wing.

▲ The gaudy plumage of the male painted bunting could hardly look more different from that of the dull, greenish female.

MUST KNOW

Wingtip feathers

There are other details that are remarkably constant. People who catch birds to band them and then release them can identify similar species by the relative lengths of their wingtip feathers—this phenomenon is known as the wing formula. In the same way that we have our middle finger longer than the others, many birds have distinctive wing formulae, so, for example, the least flycatcher (with its short wing) can be distinguished from the willow and alder flycatchers (with their moderate primary projection) and from the Acadian flycatcher (with its long wings).

Such constant patterns are vitally important to us birders as an indispensable aid to identifying individual birds; otherwise we would never succeed in the task. They allow us to find "diagnostic" differences. For instance, if we see a black-bellied or golden plover and it raises a wing to show a black "armpit," we will know immediately with 100 percent certainty that it is, in fact, a black-bellied plover. In the same way, a killdeer has two black bands across its chest, whereas a semipalmated plover has only one.

Molting

Birds do change color, and even their shape, from season to season, and as they grow from juveniles just out of the nest to being fully adult, so how do they do it? Feathers are shed, usually once or twice a year, and replaced by new ones in a process called molt. However, they don't simply fall like leaves in the fall in any old order: The process and its timing is remarkably precise.

▼ Gulls vary greatly according to age and season, but not sex, and thus present us with some interesting identification challenges.

Gulls

Take, as an example, a gull (which is big, so you can see molt in action quite easily). The young chick grows feathers in a few weeks after hatching, and it makes its first flight in this first covering of feathers, which is called "juvenile" plumage. Very soon, it replaces the feathers of its head and body, but the bigger, stronger ones of the wings and tail remain. This, the "first winter plumage," lasts through to spring. Then it replaces the feathers of its head and body once again to acquire the "first summer plumage," and begins to look more like an adult.

In the late summer and autumn, it then replaces all of its feathers for the first time—the wing and tail feathers are now a year old. The first feather to drop is the innermost "primary," one of the big feathers just behind the bend of the wing. As the complete molt continues, one primary after another is shed, so that, when the whole molt is complete, the very outermost wingtip feather is the last to grow. Because of this phenomenon, we are able to measure the progress of most birds' molt by the state of their primary feathers.

▲ Gulls, such as these, are large enough to show their feather patterns well at moderate range, so you can easily recognize when they are molting, or where there are mixed ages in one flock, as there are here.

▲ This gull chick is still in its down: It is best identified by the parent bird that comes to feed it.

▲ The male house sparrow is dull in winter, with its gray feather tips obscuring the brighter, smarter colors on the bird's head that will appear in spring.

MUST KNOW

Cardinals

Wear and tear and bleaching in the sun affect the color of birds. A cardinal in the fall will be richly colored and the red will still be intense in the spring. By late summer, its plumage is battered, pale, and dull. It hides while it molts, reappearing in late fall, fresh and bright again in a new set of feathers.

Other plumage changes

There is another way whereby color and pattern can change. Take the male house sparrow: In winter its head and breast are mottled with flecks of gray. Each feather is actually chestnut-brown or black, but with a broad grayish tip. By late winter the gray tip crumbles away, as if by some internal signal, and the chestnut-brown or black is revealed. So a winter house sparrow has a dull head pattern, but a spring one has a smart brown head side and black throat, without actually molting any feathers at all. At the same time, the bill changes from yellowish to black.

Abrasion and bleaching

Colors can change without a feather being shed in the above process—known as wear (abrasion). Feathers can also bleach: A dark feather becomes paler after several months' exposure to sunlight. Pick up feathers from a park or beach, and you may see the tip and outer edge are paler than the base and inner edge—the dark area is where the adjacent feather has covered it and kept the original color fresh and dark; the paler part shows the effects of the sun.

Note how the black wingtips of gulls turn browner with age and the effects of sun and salt. The iridescence of grackles and magpies becomes duller as the feathers get old and they lose their perfect reflections. Old feathers have slightly ragged, untidy edges; they may even be worn down to the shaft at the tip.

Pale parts of feathers are most susceptible to wear. The dark pigment is usually melanin, which not only colors a feather but also strengthens it. Going back to our gull wingtips, feathers that are black with white spots tend to lose the white parts by the end of the summer, as the white is weaker and wears away much more quickly than the black. Birds such as the American golden plover and marbled godwit have dark brown feathers with pale spots, in a dogtooth shape, along their edges in winter. By late spring, they look more uniform and dull, as the pale spots wear off, leaving all-dark feathers with sawtooth edges.

▼ This bird is a Western sandpiper in fall plumage. It is molting from its summer plumage, with red-brown on the head and wings, to the gray and white of winter. The patterned feathers on its back are summer ones, and are being replaced by new, plainer gray ones, which are easy to see.

Why different colors?

Birds can change their appearance according to their age, sex, and the season. They have evolved different colors and patterns for many reasons, the main ones, as we shall see, being advertisement for mates and camouflage.

Different requirements

Different birds have totally different requirements when it comes to color. An American white pelican, for instance, is huge: It has few obvious enemies and little need to hide. Instead, it needs to advertise its presence to other pelicans over long distances. White pelicans breed in colonies, and they also regularly band together to catch fish; together they can herd fish into the shallows where they are more easily caught. The best color to catch the eye of their colleagues is plain, bright white.

However, a female mallard makes a good meal. She must sit on the nest to incubate her eggs for weeks, so it is important to be inconspicuous. The best color for hiding away in long grass and under bushes is streaky brown. The mallard's plumage is perfect for concealment. These two extremes illustrate two entirely different requirements: Advertisement and camouflage.

▼ American white pelicans are so big that camouflage is of little use to them. They are stark white, a simple statement of their presence to other pelicans for miles around.

◄ A piping plover chick stays stock still when its parent calls; it is almost impossible to see for as long as it does not move. Any movement might give it away to a predator.

Camouflage patterning

Camouflage works for predators as well as prey. Sharp-shinned hawks can be inconspicuous when they are hiding in trees waiting for an unwary bird to come close. Camouflage patterning is known as "cryptic plumage."

Such patterns start with the egg, and thus a killdeer's egg is mottled, to break up its outline which is otherwise given away by light and shade on the smooth, curved surface. It is colored like the muddy or stony ground on which it is laid. The downy chick also has bold patterns to make it difficult for us—or a predator—to see the "round, fluffy chick." The lines and spots interfere with the shape of the chick when it stays absolutely still against a background of sand or stones, helping it to merge into the shapeless patterns around it.

The black and white bands on an adult killdeer do the same—at a glance, we can see a shapeless, incoherent patch of dark and light marks instead of the head and body of a bird. The dark color around the eye is a common feature on a bird, removing the telltale round, dark eye that will otherwise be easier to see.

MUST KNOW

Camouflage
Artists developed camouflage for warships. They were not painted dull green or blue, but a strong "dazzle" pattern to break up the ship's outline. Birds use the same technique: Their patterns look strong and obvious close-up, but become hard to see at a distance when their shape is disrupted.

MUST KNOW

Examples of camouflage

Some good examples of camouflage include birds as different as:

• Woodcocks: "Dead leaf" pattern, ideal for the woodland floor.

• Nighthawks and nightjars: Perfect for hiding against logs, desert, or open woodland floor.

• Ptarmigans: Look exactly like a lichen-covered rock. They even change with the seasons—white in winter, mottled in spring, and salt-and-pepper gray in summer to adjust to changing mountain environment.

▲ Few birds are so perfectly matched to their background as the American woodcock on a woodland floor.

Countershading

Many birds are paler underneath than they are on top. This is called "countershading." It is a very simple way to reduce the effect of light (from above) and shade (below) which could otherwise highlight the shape of a bird against a flat background. Instead, we see the dark area lit from above, and the pale area in shade below, creating a flatter, more uniform effect.

Some birds, such as the common snipe in marshes, effectively "disappear" against their typical habitats. Even the upper edge of the flank on a Swainson's thrush or song sparrow, for example, which often catches the light, is a fraction darker than the rest of the underparts to minimize the effect of sunlight from above.

Advertising colors

"Right is might" in most cases when male birds threaten each other. The male on his territory usually succeeds in driving away an intruder, but should he then cross the boundary, the positions are reversed. The white shield on the forehead of a coot, when shown off by a bird

▲ Female barn swallows prefer male birds which have long tails and sleek, richly colored plumage.

bowing its head down just above the water surface, is usually enough to defuse the situation and settle matters without coming to blows. Thus colors play a huge part in reducing the need for physical attacks. If an unpaired male bird with no territory is determined to claim a space, however, fighting may ensue—American coots very occasionally fight to the death. Male coots will fight other male coots and female coots can fight off female intruders.

▼ Adult Northern gannets are vivid white: They fight and use aggressive displays in the breeding colony. Young gannets, once they have grown out of their first covering of down, are dark to help them avoid being attacked by an adult, which could be fatal.

Coloring of young birds

Too immature to breed, young birds are not seeking a mate or a territory, so they have no need to advertise their colors. They are better off being dull and inconspicuous. Hence we see brown-streaked young gulls and mottled American robins lacking the intense red color of the breast.

Kittiwakes and gannets

Young black-legged kittiwakes are hatched in tiny nests on minute ledges, at a dizzy height above the sea. Above all they must not be knocked off the ledge before they can fly. If an intruding adult is at the nest, the rightful owner will attack. Adult kittiwakes have immaculate white heads. To avoid being attacked by mistake, a young one has a broad black band on its neck, which it displays to its incoming parent: "Don't peck, it's me!" Similarly, young northern gannets are blackish; adult gannets, which are pure white, are especially aggressive at their nest toward other adult gannets and a youngster must avoid being speared by another gannet's beak at all costs.

▲ Young black-legged kittiwakes have bold black markings to help distinguish them from trespassing adults.

▼ Black-legged kittiwakes nest on tiny ledges high above the sea.

Leaving the nest

It is a tough world for young birds once they have left the nest and become independent of their parents. They must learn hunting or feeding skills quickly, and must do so in competition with other birds; if they fail, they will soon die. Many, including some woodpeckers and owls, must find a territory and defend it almost immediately; otherwise they, too, may starve.

Young birds of migratory species have to set off for their wintering areas within a few weeks of fledging, and travel without any map, help, or previous knowledge. Small birds, such as finches, sparrows, and chickadees, become mature enough to breed at one year old. There is little or no chance to spend time "growing up" for most birds.

▲ This juvenile herring gull will become independent within a few days.

Postures and displays

Birds use stereotyped physical actions, as well as their colors, in communicating with each other and with other species. Display is body language, or communication by posture or movement, in a stereotyped or ritual way. All displays must be "standardized" for each species so that other individuals can recognize them and know exactly what they mean. That means you, too, can begin to read the signs.

Submissive displays

A bird in a submissive pose is saying the same thing as a dog with its tail between its legs: "I give in, so don't hurt me." These postures help to avoid a fight. Females use submissive poses when pairing with males, overcoming the natural tendency for any close encounter to end in a fight. Birds have their "individual space," which is not to be invaded by other birds, but courtship has to break down such built-in barriers.

▼ Violent though this looks, a mute swan confrontation is not especially serious. Most bird skirmishes are far more about posturing and jostling than actual combat.

Ritualized displays

It is easy to see ritualized displays: Just visit your local park and watch the ducks. From fall through late spring, male ducks often gather together and display communally; there is much shaking of the head or tail, wing-flapping, stretching, or preening movements. It looks like the birds are just keeping comfortable, but in fact all these are valid displays, with meaning to other ducks.

Any colony of birds will always be full of posturing and displaying. Gulls, for example, often point their heads up in a gesture of challenge, or face away in appeasement. If frustrated, they might even tug at a piece of grass or other material. Such displays may reduce aggression within a tightly-packed community, or reinforce pair bonds, which are essential for the successful rearing of a family in many species. Few birds will normally allow another bird to touch them—they like to keep their own space. Yet, to breed, they must be able to come together in an intimate way, to feed each other and their chicks. They have to develop trust and, at least for a few weeks, a strong bond between the sexes.

▲ The somewhat dowdy blue grouse becomes a spectacular sight during its display. It also gives off very low-pitched hooting sounds.

MUST KNOW

Threat displays
You can easily see birds' displays, even from your window. One kind is a simple threat: "Come closer and I'll peck you." Purple and house finches will often squabble on a feeder using threat postures, such as thrusting the head forward with the beak open.

House sparrows

Male house sparrows add weight to their plumage patterns (the one with the biggest black bib is most likely to win a mate) by their postures. They do not sing much, but scuttle over the ground with head up, tail raised, body pressed down and wings half-spread, to impress watching females.

Red-winged blackbirds

One of the easiest displays to see is the flashing of the epaulettes of the red-winged blackbird, the posture that accompanying its emphatic song. The epaulettes are ruffled as the bird partially opens its wings. This display is territorial rather than to attract a mate. Individuals whose epaulettes were experimentally darkened were less likely to acquire or hold on to a territory than unaffected birds, whereas their ability to attract females was unimpaired. Birds in their own territories perform their display brazenly, but should they intrude into another bird's territory, perhaps to feed, they keep their red "badges" well covered to prevent attack.

Northern cardinals

If you watch carefully, it is possible to follow the Northern cardinal's courtship progress in spring. The first thing you'll probably notice is two birds feeding side-by-side on the feeding station,

▲ Here is a male house sparrow in spring, his black bib at its most extensive. He looks fit, strong, and a suitable father for healthy chicks, so a female might select him instead of a male with a smaller bib.

▼ It's hard to miss the flashing red display of the territory-holding male red-winged blackbird.

without any of their species' usual bickering. This ease with each other will move into singing, with the male taking the lead phrases, followed by the female echoing the phrase. As nesting time gets close, the male will bring deliveries of food to the female, and pass them to her bill-to-bill. And finally, at its most intense phase, courtship is a private ceremony that most people have never seen: Each member of the pair leans to one side, then the other, in a swaying motion known as the "lopsided" pose. This often leads to copulation.

▲ Pairs of mourning doves are often openly affectionate, cuddling up together and preening each other.

Mourning doves

Mourning doves are not shy about courting; you can often see them on roofs or aerials, cuddled up together and preening each other adoringly, like two unselfconscious adolescents. This mutual preening, or "allopreening," is common among many birds, and is a little similar to the mutual delousing performed by some monkeys and apes.

Allopreening is not so much courtship—in which a male makes an initial attempt to attract a female—but is more about pair maintenance. Mourning doves pair for the long term, and this attractive display helps them to synchronize their breeding cycle.

MUST KNOW

Hummingbird displays

Each species has its own display, which can be used to identify it. The best known of these is the early spring "pendulum display" of the ruby-throated hummer. The male flies rapidly from side to side, following the course of a somewhat fiercely swinging pendulum.

Size

It is hard to judge a bird's size. Most things naturally look bigger at close range, but often what seems to be a "big bird" far away becomes quite small when it is seen close up. Common backyard birds, such as black-capped chickadees, are tiny, while a kinglet would fit into the palm of your hand, so it's not surprising that you may struggle to see details from 50 yards.

MUST KNOW

Big or small
Birds are usually chicken-sized or less; few are goose-sized or above. Giants include the California condor, black-footed albatross, whooping crane, and wood stork, which have wingspans well in excess of the height of a tall man. The smallest are the hummingbirds, of which the calliope is only 3.25" long.

Weight versus length

The common measure of size in identification books is the measurement from bill tip to tail tip, which gives little idea of bulk. A very slim, long-bodied bird, such as a greater yellowlegs, is the same length as a short-billed, heavily-built one, such as a rock ptarmigan, but will look much smaller. A herring gull is only a few inches longer than a ring-billed gull, but may be so much more heavily built that, side by side, it may look "twice as big." Weight is often a better clue than length as appearances can be deceptive.

▶ The books would have you believe that a yellowlegs is as big as a ptarmigan—but of course, it is much smaller, neater, and more elegant.

Big birds

These are generally more relaxed, using much less energy, eating large meals at long intervals (such as the vultures and eagles), or constantly swallowing large amounts of low-nutrition food, as do geese and swans, which are among the few grazers of grass and leaves.

Small birds

Many small birds live frenetic lives, really living on their nerves: They have a fast heartbeat, a high body temperature, and a high metabolic rate. Such short-lived, high-speed creatures are not suited to being a very large size—they need a constant intake of food just to keep them going.

▲ A typical large raptor with broad wings and tail, the bald eagle can soar effortlessly. But it is quite a versatile hunter, well able to catch food by plunging its feet into the water.

Shapes

These are associated with lifestyles, foraging, evading predators, and habitats. For waterfowl, they are broad-bodied, boat-shaped birds, with a natural double-bend to the head and neck so the neck is erect and the head horizontal.

Swans

These large birds feed on submerged vegetation and, to reach it, need their long necks. They also "upend" with head thrust even deeper into the water and tail upright, held in position by paddling their broadly-webbed feet. They graze on dry land, but are big, heavy, plodding birds with short legs, so they are not very agile and nave no real need to be. They take off from water with a short run across the surface, pattering with their feet.

Geese

These are more terrestrial than swans, walking more easily on longer legs, and grazing or pecking at roots and leaves with their stouter beaks. They have medium-length, sinuous necks to help them

► The long neck of the trumpeter swan enables it to reach food on the bottom, even in quite deep water.

do this but have no need for the very long, slender necks that swans have. They take off much more easily than swans, with a direct leap from land or a short patter across water.

▲ Ducks, like these wood ducks, have shorter necks and smaller bodies than swans and feed at the surface. In ducks, the male and female usually look dissimilar to each other.

Ducks

Ducks come in several subgroups. Some have broad, flat bills, with fine filters along each side, which are designed to sieve seeds and tiny creatures from a "soup" of muddy water: These are the "dabbling ducks." They can upend, but rarely dive; some, such as the familiar mallard and American wigeon, will also graze quite happily on land.

Other ducks, such as eiders and scoters, have deeper bills, with which they crunch small shellfish and crustaceans. Redheads and ring-necked ducks have broader bills for coping with small mollusks and plant material. Mergansers have longer bills with a sharp hook at the tip and serrated edges, which are designed for dealing with slippery fish. All of these ducks feed underwater, diving down from the surface: They are "diving ducks."

▲ The long bill of this snipe is flexible and sensitive at the tip, making it ideal for probing deeply and form grasping food in soft mud.

Shorebirds

Another large group shaped by lifestyle is the shorebirds, including plovers and sandpipers. Most are waterside birds, feeding in muddy places or in or beside shallow water. The length of their legs and bills helps define their roles and the food that they concentrate on.

Long bills

Curlews and whimbrels have long, downcurved bills for probing into crevices for crabs or pushing deep into soft mud for marine worms or other invertebrates. Godwits and dowitchers, however, simply probe their straight bills into the mud.

Snipe do the same in muddy places by freshwater. They have sensitive and flexible bill tips that can not only feel worms but also open slightly—they can grab and swallow a worm underground. While they are doing this, they need to be aware of potential danger: Snipes and American woodcocks have large eyes set so far back on their heads that they can see behind them while they feed. With their specialist detection equipment, probing deep into the ground, they have no need to look forward.

Shorter bills

Red knots, dunlins, sanderlings, and various species of sandpipers, among other shorebirds have shorter bills, but they are still fairly long and thin. They pick from the surface, or probe with quick, shallow pinpricks, taking tiny food from the surface of the mud or just below it. Plovers are even shorter-billed. The semipalmated and piping plovers pick their food from the ground without probing. Turnstones have thicker bills, flat on top and slightly upcurved beneath—ideal for slipping beneath pebbles and lumps of stranded seaweed, which are tossed over to reveal tiny insects and crustaceans.

▲ The American avocet has a remarkable beak. It is swept upward and flattened toward the tip, so that, as the bird leans forward, it can be swept sideways just below the surface of salty water or semi-liquid mud.

◄ Shorebirds come in many different sizes, with different lengths of leg and differently shaped bills, so that many species can feed in the same habitat but competition is reduced.

Unusual birds

The black-necked stilt is closely related to the avocet but does things differently. Its enormously long legs mean it can wade into deeper water, but has a shorter, straight bill for picking insects from the surface with delicacy and precision.

Beaks

Beaks (or bills) are used for several tasks, such as preening (putting the vanes of disarranged feathers back together and removing dust and feather mites), drinking, and building nests. Their principal day-to-day use, however, is feeding, and it is this that shapes them.

Unusual bills

Some birds have remarkable bills. Few are more outlandish than that of the black skimmer, whose lower mandible is much longer than the upper mandible. The skimmer has a unique feeding method, in which it flies just above the water with the bill open and the lower jaw plowing through the surface. Food is located by touch and caught by the upper mandible snapping down on it. Pelicans have famously large bills with flexible pouches that can scoop up large volumes of water, which is then expelled, while the bird hangs on tightly to any fish that it has caught. The puffins have very deep, narrow bills that are colorful for display purposes and enable the birds to carry many fish at once.

◀ A pelican uses its large bill to scoop up water and fish into its soft, extendable pouch. It squeezes out the water and swallows the fish. This is a brown pelican.

Hooked bills

Raptors and owls have hooked bills, to help tear up prey. Falcons have a "tooth" or notch on the edge of the upper mandible, to help dispatch prey with a strong nip to the neck. Most raptors kill with their feet and use their bills for feeding.

▲ The falcon's bill has a distinctive hooked tip, which makes it useful for tearing its prey into bite-sized bits.

Other bills

● Wood warblers have slim bills to probe into foliage and pick up fragile insects.

● Flycatchers, including pewees, phoebes, and kingbirds, have broader beaks, fringed with stiff bristles to snap up insects in flight.

● Swallows and martins have small bills, but wide mouths which help catch insects in mid-air.

● Thrashers have long, curved bills that sweep sideways in the litter, making "thrashing" noises.

● Meadowlarks have thin bills for probing into the ground and then opening, making a hole.

● Robins and thrushes have stout beaks for pulling up worms or probing for invertebrates among leaf litter; they are tough enough to pluck berries.

● Waxwings have small but wide bills with a large gape for eating berries.

● Hummingbirds have enormously long bills which they insert into flowerheads to sip nectar.

● Woodpeckers have strong, chisel-shaped bills for hammering into tree bark.

● Finches have strong, quite stout bills to deal with strong seeds, but there is much variation.

Legs and feet

Legs and feet vary just as much as beaks. Most birds have a standard three toes forward, one back pattern, but a few, such as the fast-running sanderling, have just three toes. Leg length also varies greatly, from the tiny, almost useless legs of swifts, with four tiny forward-facing toes, to the enormously long ones of cranes and stilts.

Swimming birds

Mostly, these have webbed feet. Ducks' feet have three toes joined by webs and a free hind toe, but cormorants, pelicans, and anhingas have all four toes webbed. Coots, grebes, and loons have a different foot, with their toes broadly lobed. When swimming, the lobes are wide open to present the greatest possible thrust on the backstroke, but on the forward stroke they fold back, closed to minimize drag.

▼ Although large and heavy, the common eider duck is quite streamlined and has webbed feet, ideal for swimming in the sea and underwater.

◄ Cormorants (here a great cormorant), like pelicans, have all their four toes connected by broad webs, giving them additional propulsion when swimming and diving underwater.

Wading birds

These birds have long, fine toes, which are useful for spreading the bird's weight on soft mud. Moorhens, purple gallinules, and the rare Northern jacana have particularly long toes, helping them to walk on floating vegetation. They do not need the broad lobes of the coot, as they seldom if ever dive deeply for food and they swim much less often.

▼ The common moorhen is a good all-rounder, swimming, climbing, and walking, and its long toes are particularly suited for spreading its weight on semi-floating vegetation.

Diurnal raptors

These birds have strong, muscular, tough-scaled feet. Their toes have sharp, curved claws, or talons, for holding and killing prey. However, not all conform to this basic pattern. The New World vultures do not generally kill their food, and they have fairly long legs for walking on the ground, with short claws that are not especially sharp. The Northern caracara is primarily a terrestrial scavenger. Ospreys have stubby toes equipped with sharp scales, to help them grasp slippery fish, and huge, arched claws. They can reverse the outer toe, so instead of the usual pattern of three forward, one back, they have two forward, two back (or one to the side) to give a better grip.

◀ The crested caracara is an unusual raptor, often feeding on carrion or digging up insects from the ground.

▼ An osprey has short, powerful toes but extremely long, hooked claws and spiky scales on the soles of its feet, to give extra grip on a slippery fish.

Other birds

Woodpeckers, owls, and parrots also have two toes forward, two toes back: This "zygodactyl" pattern is also shown by cuckoos. Kingfishers have two toes fused at the base, to help them shovel loose earth backward as they burrow their long nesting tunnels. Puffins do the same thing and have the inner claw sharp and incurved to help them dig.

Songbirds with three forward toes and one hind toe have special tendons that help them to grip a perch as they rest their weight upon it and flex the leg. Those that run through long grass, such as pipits, longspurs, and meadowlarks, tend to have very long hind claws.

▲ The outer toe of this golden-fronted woodpecker is turned backwards, so as to provide a wider, stronger grip on curved branches and tree trunks.

Calls and song

Not only are birds' plumage patterns surprisingly constant, according to their species, age, season, and sex, but each species has characteristic calls, or vocalizations, which help us to identify them. They are distinctive because, in most cases, they are intended to communicate something to other individuals of the same species, and therefore they must be recognizably different from each others' sounds.

Alarm calls

Some calls are specific to males, females, or young birds, in the same way that each has its own plumage. Most birds will have several calls and usually one or two can be recognized easily whereas others may be confusingly difficult to identify: These are typically "alarm calls," which warn of approaching danger.

Alarm calls given by small woodland birds are high-pitched and thin, with no strong consonant sounds—a simple "sseeeee." This penetrating sound can be heard within a wood, warning of the approach of a sharp-shinned hawk, say, but the lack of hard elements makes it extremely difficult to pinpoint. The bird can give the call without revealing its position to the hawk. Hard-ended notes are more easily located.

Contact calls

Other bird calls (or "notes") include "contact calls" which help families or winter flocks or migrating groups to stay together. They are more or less "conversational," and are given every so often to reassure others: "I'm still here," or "follow me."

Typical contact calls are short and simple, such as the hard "tick" of the Northern cardinal, or the mew of a catbird. Almost everyone knows the clucking of a robin, the caw of an American crow, or the ringing "kew" of a flicker.

MUST KNOW

Unusual calls
Birds utter all kinds of calls, and these may begin in the egg. Many yet-to-hatch chicks make soft sounds to their parent. Later on, the parents recognize the calls of their young, and this helps to locate them.

▲ The yellow-headed blackbird is famous for having what is probably the worst song of any North American bird—it sounds rather like a chainsaw!

Flight calls

Contact calls merge into flight calls, which are obviously given in flight and are very useful in our bird recognition. So, an evening grosbeak calls a slightly hoarse "clee-ip" call, a purple finch a metallic "pick," while an American goldfinch utters a lighter "ti-dee-di-di." Any one of these might fly over your backyard, and the best way to know them is by their call.

Shorebirds have especially distinctive calls, which are vital in identification: The yellowlegs, for example, are hard to distinguish except by call (greater yellowlegs give three to four emphatic "dew-dew-dews," while the lesser only calls one to two softer "tip" notes) and, to the practiced ear, the dowitchers are more easily distinguishable by sound (long-billed are higher-pitched than short-billed) than by anything else. The ear picks out the rising "peet-weet" of the solitary sandpiper and distinguishes it from the falling "peet-weet-weet" of the spotted. Such calls from shorebirds convey alarm, too, when they are given in a louder, more intense form.

▲ Distinguishing the two species of yellowlegs by sight is difficult (this is a greater yellowlegs), but their calls are more helpful.

Young birds

Young birds call to be fed; the pleading sounds of robins and chickadees can be heard in any summer backyard, with their feeble yet penetrating quality. Adults give warning calls to make their chicks keep stock still. Male raptorial birds call to a female on the nest to say: "I'm coming in, with food."

Bird song

Song is the most complex and developed kind of vocal communication. Most species have a distinct song. Some are simple and stereotyped, whereas others are more complex but with little individual variation. Yet others, such as the song of the wood thrush or brown thrasher, maintain the recognizable character of the species but involve individual improvisation and great variety.

The repetitive tapping "tick-tick, tick-tick-tick…" of the yellow rail is a song in terms of its function, but it is not musical—bird song is not necessarily musical in a human sense. It lets other birds know the singer is there. In territorial species, other males know that the territory is occupied.

At the same time, females are attracted to the song of a male. They can even make an assessment of his qualities as a potential mate, simply by listening. In many birds, males with the most elaborate repertoires prove to have the greatest success in attracting a mate.

When to hear song

Song is especially concentrated early in the breeding season when it is most intense for mate attraction and territorial defense. Also early in the day and again at dusk—in spring and early summer a "dawn chorus" in a woodland is unforgettable. However, birds will often sing through the day and sometimes even at night, especially in habitats such as marshland, where they are accustomed not to be able to see each other. And, of course, owls and nightjars, such as whip-poor-wills and nighthawks, also sing and call in the darkness.

Copying sounds

Song is largely inherited, but in the best songsters it is also partly learned, or copied. The Northern mockingbird, an astonishingly good mimic, will

include in its song fragments of vocalizations of many birds that it hears roundabout, incorporating them in single song bouts that may last half an hour or more. The mockingbird is not just an accomplished singer, it is a tireless one, too.

Mockers add phrases to their repertoire all the time, and discard others. Many include other environmental sounds, such as the howl of a coyote or, more mundanely, sounds like dog barks, bells, and human whistles. Increased complexity tells others that this is a mature, experienced, fit bird, not to be trifled with—and potentially a father of strong, healthy offspring.

▲ In the breeding season the Northern mockingbird may sing incessantly all day and all night long.

Learning bird calls

If you want to learn some bird sounds, start out in late winter and early spring, when fewer birds are singing and deciduous trees are not yet in leaf. Once the migrants have arrived you will be completely confused. You'll be surprised how important it is to look at a bird when you are trying to learn its song; somehow the aural and visual images complement and enhance one another. When you are starting, get a handle on the distinctive ones first: The "Old Sam Peabody" of the white-throated sparrow, or the "Drink your teeeeee" of the Eastern towhee, and the sighing song of the black-capped chickadee.

Sounds are difficult to learn because they can't readily be picked up from a fieldguide. The guides help as much as they can, but it is hard to say "tik k jijijijijiji-jrr" and learn a marsh wren, or say "tsweewf" and know it is a verdin. Then you have to remember which sound comes from which bird, and that can be daunting.

Learn songs before calls. Songs are more complex and have a territorial meaning; they are the bird's signature tunes. Calls are much briefer, with fewer clues and less time to assimilate them. Many birds just go "chip" or "tick," and only considerable time in the field can sort these out.

▲ When learning bird sounds, the rule is the same as for sight identification: Start by getting thoroughly familiar with common birds, such as the song sparrow.

◄ The clear song of the Eastern meadowlark soon becomes familiar to those living in rural farming areas.

Start with familiar birds

Initiate yourself by learning the songs or calls of your backyard birds, the ones that you hear most frequently and have the best chance of remembering. And learn them thoroughly before expanding your horizons. The American robin, for example, has a slightly rushed singing style that is similar to that of several other species, and you'll need to know it well. But you will be making progress if you have picked up the songs of the cardinal and house wren, the nasal call of the white-breasted nuthatch, the coo of the mourning dove, or the harsh call of the common grackle or Brewer's blackbird.

Use descriptive terms, such as "squeal," "shout," "sharp," "metallic," and "mellow," to try to describe the sounds that you hear. Write them down if you possibly can—even peculiar notations ("speez," "swairnk," "titki-too") to help fix sounds in your mind. You might draw a line above the word, rising and falling over each syllable to show any variation in pitch. Make your own fieldguide! Once you know sounds, you will react to them. And the more sounds you learn, the easier it is to add more all the time.

▲ Even shorebirds on the beach each have distinctive calls that help us to identify them in flight.

want to know more?

Take it to the next level...

Go to...
▶ **Habitats for birds** page 116
▶ **Use your records** page 182
▶ **Join a club** page 186

Other sources
▶ **CDs and DVDs**
   for top-quality bird song recordings
▶ **Bird magazines**
   look for ads for bird song tapes
▶ **Bird song tapes**
   for playing in the car on long journeys
▶ **Fieldguides**
   for illustrations of bird shapes, etc.
▶ **Publications**
   visit www.buteobooks.com for bird books

habitats

for birds

You will soon notice that while certain birds live in particular areas near you, they do not live elsewhere—each species has its own favored habitat. A habitat is defined as the sum of the characteristics of the area in which a bird lives, including the vegetation, nest sites, roosting sites, food, and feeding areas, as well as the weather and the altitude.

▶

What is a habitat?

Many bird species are generalists and can make a living in a surprising variety of places. Even so, they have their special needs and, if these are lost, they disappear. Others are specialists and it is much easier to see how they are tied to a particular habitat and way of life.

A means of survival

It was only in 1903 that the Kirtland's warbler's nesting grounds were found, in central Michigan. Since its first discovery in 1851, it has always been rare and mysterious. It has evolved to take advantage of one specific habitat, and nothing else. Centuries ago, wildfires burned woodland patches every year, so there were always patches of jack pines five or six years old, with grassy clearings, somewhere: exactly what Kirtland's warblers must have. Once the trees grew too tall, they would simply move to another patch of the right age. Since people controlled wildfires and turned most woodland into farmland, chances of finding suitable jack pine plots have been almost nil. Now, the birds

▼ Seventy per cent of Kirtland's warblers return to their breeding grounds, but only 36 per cent of the juveniles survive migration to and from the Caribbean. The key to increasing their numbers is to increase the area of suitable habitat.

survive only where people deliberately manage stands of pine to meet their needs.

In 1951, there were 432 singing males. By 1961, this increased to 502, but by 1971 there had been a sharp fall to 201: The species seemed to be heading out. By 1995, there had been a recovery and 765 were found, in just six Michigan counties.

Brown-headed cowbirds only recently spread into Kirtland's warbler habitat and the warblers were not adapted to defend against them. The cowbirds parasitize numerous species and don't particularly need Kirtland's. As the warblers declined, the cowbirds could still increase. By 1980, more than 40,000 cowbirds had been removed, and Kirtland's fledging rates tripled. Cowbird control and habitat management has, for the moment, saved the day for this warbler with its exceptionally narrow habitat needs.

Yet, the future is still uncertain. We need to maintain enough habitat in Michigan for Kirtland's warblers to survive without constant human interference, and we must also protect the habitat in its winter quarters in the West Indies.

▲ With its fussy ecological requirements, the Kirtland's warbler maintains a perilously low world population. Its problems have been compounded in recent years by brown-headed cowbirds laying their eggs in its nests; these parasitic birds now have to be controlled in Kirtland's warbler breeding areas.

▲ American dippers are found only near water. They nest under banks overhanging water and feed alongside and under the water; without it, they cannot survive.

Specialist habitats

The American dipper is a unique songbird that wades into water, swims on the surface, and even dives underneath. It uses its long, sharp claws to get a grip on the bottom and leans forward so the flow of the water pushes it down. Its diet exploits the abundance of insect larvae and crustaceans in freshwater torrents—food that is out of reach of most birds.

It has to be running fresh water, preferably with a few overhanging trees and stony shallows where it can perch on a boulder. It makes its nest under an overhang above the water. Take it out of this environment and the dipper is lost: It can't feed in any other way.

Similarly, the brown creeper searches tree bark for insects and makes a good living at it, but it really cannot do much else. Now and then one may forage on a rocky outcrop or an old stone wall, but basically the brown creeper clings to bark, using its tail as a prop, creeps

Demanding habitats

Species that have adapted to live in demanding habitats may not be able to live elsewhere. While a song sparrow can perch in a tree or hop about on the ground, a seaside sparrow probably never perches in a tree in its life. Instead it runs around on the ground, mouse-like, among salt-marsh grass, where it lives and breeds. A bird that has adapted to a demanding habitat cannot go back.

upward in a spiral, then flies to the foot of the next tree and starts again. It has long, needle-sharp, arched claws, a stiff tail, and a fine, curved bill that are all ideal for the job, but is practically unable to stand or walk on level ground.

Dependence on habitat

Birds' dependence on a specific habitat is absolute, and understanding such relationships helps in conservation. The Cassin's sparrow of the desert grasslands of the south does not just depend on its tall grass habitat to survive. It must also time its breeding season to coincide with the annual late summer rains, when the plants of the desert set seed. If it times its breeding wrong, or the rains fail, its chicks will starve.

Warblers

In his famous study of the warblers of the Northern conifer forest, the late Robert MacArthur found that each of five widespread species, the Cape May, yellow-rumped, black-throated green, Blackburnian, and bay-breasted, used a slightly different part of the same habitat to the other species, at least when all were present. The Cape May warbler mostly foraged in the treetops, while the yellow-rumped warbler did so in the lower branches of the same trees.

Bitterns

American bitterns are brilliantly adapted to live
in tall, dense marsh grass above water, using
their huge toes to cling to stems or balance their
weight as they lean forward, looking for fish. But
the vegetation must be right—well camouflaged
as they are, bitterns prefer not to venture out
into the open and usually feed on the edge of a
bank of vegetation or well hidden inside it. The
fish have to come to them. So the right type of
marsh grass must be wet enough to allow fish to
swim inside, or have narrow ditches and creeks
of open water overshadowed by tall vegetation.

▼ Bitterns must have
reedbeds; when they stand
still and stretch themselves
upright, they even look like
a bunch of reeds.

◀ In the early years of the 21st century, many common murres have found it harder to find food, such as sand lances, and have sometimes failed to rear any young. Their relationship with the sea and its abundance of fish has changed drastically, probably because of rapid climate change.

These habitats have a natural tendency to dry out and turn into scrub, and we have to maintain healthy marshland environments by expensive management and manipulation of water tables.

Complex relationships

Birds have complex relationships with their habitats, including food supplies. Even seabirds, which go to sea to find fish and nest on cliffs by the ocean, have intricate relationships with water temperatures, plankton, and fish populations, that together make up or influence the web of life in the ocean. With global warming it is possible that many populations of alcids and other northern breeding seabirds will be squeezed as their staple foods move north in response to the rise in sea temperature, leaving many colonies abandoned. These problems are exacerbated by overfishing (e.g. on the Grand Banks of Newfoundland, where the population of capelin has crashed), and pollution, as in the disastrous oil spillage by the Exxon Valdez tanker off Alaska in 1989.

MUST KNOW

Food webs

Birds can thrive only if their complicated food webs are also thriving. These may start with just tiny organisms in the soil, which are devoured by small insects, then larger insects, or soil nutrients that allow plants to grow which produce food for insects and set seed. The seedbanks in the soils of much of our agricultural land has been depleted by intensive farming and modern fields can be almost devoid of birds.

Changes in habitat

Birds have to find enough to eat, day after day, in the small area in which they live. They need nest sites, roosting sites, and safe places to hide when they are threatened. Take away any of these and most birds are unable to cope. They have been adapting to specialized ways of living for millions of year and they cannot change now.

▲ Farmland habitats have always changed but only in recent decades has such change been so fast and so dramatic that birds have been affected severely. Fields of wheat and barley stubble, left all winter after harvesting and full of seeds for hungry birds, are now rarely seen.

Changes in the land

At the beginning of the 20th century, business was booming for many North American farmland birds. Large-scale deforestation had vastly increased their available habitat, and a good many species, from grassland specialists such as the dickcissel, to edge species such as brown-headed cowbirds, were able either to expand their ranges or to surge in numbers. At the beginning of this century, 100 years later, things have turned around completely. The majority of farmland birds are in decline, many of them severely. Even totemic open country birds, such as the ubiquitous red-winged blackbird, are falling in numbers.

Intensification

Why are birds that live on the outskirts of farmland in decline? In a word, intensification is the problem. This is an umbrella term for the various changes wrought by the need for higher yield from the same plot of land. So, for example, those small edges that were refuges for birds, such as patches of brush or even wet ditches, are now increasingly being destroyed and brought under the plow.

The less economic farming practices, including diversification, are being surrendered to monoculture agriculture. And, finally, the land is being fed more and more in the way of fertilizers, herbicides, and pesticides, making it a clean, chemical environment which is lacking in any diversity.

Who knows, too, what genetically modified (GM) farming will bring? At the time of writing, there is contradictory evidence about whether this will benefit wildlife or harm it, and the threats to our birds are unknown?

▼ Grassland, such as this, is one of North America's most threatened habitats.

Changing habitats

Migration can help many species to cope with the demands of survival. Shorebirds in the nonbreeding season can feed on an abundance of tiny worms, mollusks, and crustaceans in the mud of an estuary or delta, where there may be tens of thousands of minute organisms in a square meter of surface mud, enriched twice daily by the incoming tides. They spread out to feed as the tide recedes, but must withdraw as the water rises and move off to a safe place to roost during the high tide period.

This pattern varies during each month according to the level of the tides: Spring tides cover even the highest parts of the beach and make feeding impossible, while neap tides leave so much exposed that the birds may continue feeding all day. High tides also occur at any time of day or night, so shorebirds must be able to feed at dusk or dawn or even at night, or by day. They have to adapt to changing circumstances.

But very few shorebirds breed in these habitats. Most move at least to inland bogs and grassland, or along rivers, and the great majority fly off to the Arctic, to breed there as soon as

MUST KNOW

The seasons
Great movements of millions of birds across the earth have been stimulated by the changing seasons. Opportunities exist in the north in summer, which birds take advantage of, but to avoid the severe weather in the north, they have to move south to the Southern States, or Central and South America.

▼ Some shorebirds breed in the far north and winter south as far as the southern parts of South America. These are semipalmated sandpipers.

conditions allow, which may not be until June. They and their growing chicks feed on millions of summer bugs, including mosquitoes and their larvae from the shallow pools.

▲ Dunlins nest in the tundra, especially in wet, marshy areas. In winter, though, they exchange this habitat for tidal flats and beaches.

Contrasting habitats

Many birds have different habitats according to the season, and some of the same species may have various habitats that differ greatly from each other. Examples include the piping plover, which breeds on sandy beaches in the northeast and on shingle or lakeshores in the prairies, and the willet, which is confined to saltwater in the northwest but occurs in freshwater habitats elsewhere.

Swifts are remarkable birds whose habitat is essentially open air, for most of their lives. They feed and may even sleep in the air for many months of the year, and some species (e.g. the chimney swift) migrate to South America for the winter, constantly remaining airborne. For a brief period of the year the swifts need access to breeding sites, such as chimneys, rock crevices, and trees, but their brief breeding season dalliance with solid platforms echoes the habits of seabirds coming to land to breed.

▶

Backyard birds

Most of us have access to a yard, or to a town park. These habitats attract forest-edge birds that have adapted to a way of life close to people, often supported by householders who put out food (deliberately or unwittingly) and nestboxes.

▲ The splendid pyrrhuloxia is a relative of the Northern cardinal which only occurs in the southwestern United States, visiting backyards, and in northern Mexico.

Location matters

What you see depends on where you are. Some birds, such as mourning doves and juncos, can be found in backyards almost throughout North America, but a good many others are more restricted to specific habitats and regions.

Blue jays and Northern cardinals, for example, are mainly eastern birds, while Steller's jays and Cassin's finches are almost unknown there, but common in the western states. More exotic feeder visitors in the southern states include such birds as painted buntings, pyrrhuloxias, and California towhees.

Even a window ledge is enough for a rock dove, a descendant of a wild bird that originally nested on cliffs and mountains—cities are its adopted home. You could also attract house sparrows, and the slightly less urban areas will attract house finches or even the occasional black-capped chickadee. In fact, all of these small species have been seen on hanging feeders high up in skyscrapers in our cities.

Backyard visitors

Even a moderate-sized backyard with just a lawn, some shrubs, a few trees, and a bird feeding station will bring in quite a variety of visitors. As stated above, what you see will depend a lot on where you live—the habitat and climate of your region. In the following pages, we shall take a look at a selection of our commoner bird species.

Chickadees and titmice

Almost everyone in North America has visits from one sort of chickadee or another, be it a black-capped chickadee over much of the continent, a Carolina chickadee in the southeast, a mountain chickadee in the Rockies, or a chestnut-backed chickadee along the Pacific coast. They all feed eagerly both at platform feeders and hanging feeders, and they can all be encouraged to use artificial boxes, although black-capped chickadees, for one, prefer to excavate their own nest hole and use them sparingly. The less boldly marked titmice are equally common visitors to feeders and, indeed, so enthusiastically do tufted titmice take to backyard food supplies that their range has expanded northwards as the trend in bird feeding has increased.

Finches

Our backyards play host of a range of colorful finches, and most people who put up feeders will attract several species. Finches are highly specialized seedeaters, and most have a groove in the upper mandible in which they lodge a seed, then bring the lower mandible to bear on the husk and, using the tongue, peel the husk from the kernel. This is called mandibulation, and you can often see finches doing this as they sit on the perches of tube feeders.

The size and shape of a finch's bill is suitable for eating different seeds. Evening grosbeaks have very deep, powerful bills and soon tuck into sunflower seeds; goldfinches, however, have thin bills which are actually adapted to feeding from thistleheads—tiny niger seeds will attract them from miles around. Pine siskins are related to goldfinches and also favor the smaller seeds.

The most common finches in many backyards are the more modestly colored purple finches and house finches. Although

▲ Once confined to the southwest, house finches were released into New York City in the 1940s and found the backyards there very much to their liking. They have since thrived, and now occur almost throughout the entire continent.

closely related, they do not flock together; but they can often be seen on platform feeders together. Surprisingly, despite their smaller size, house finches are usually dominant over their more timid relatives.

▲ The dark-eyed junco, in all its various forms (this is the southwestern gray-headed version) visits bird feeding stations almost throughout the continent.

Juncos and sparrows

Cornell University's FeederWatcher program recently found that the most widespread and frequent visitor to North American backyard feeding stations was the dark-eyed junco, in all its various forms, from the widespread slate-colored version to the Oregon version in the west, and the gray-headed race in the southwest. These birds are most familiar in winter in many areas, and are sometimes nicknamed "snowbirds." But they can come to backyards at any time of year, attracted by an abundant supply of seeds. They prefer not to use platforms or hanging feeders, but are most at home on the ground.

Juncos and sparrows feed on smaller seeds than finches. To feed, they do not de-husk their seeds in the manner of a finch, but crush them instead, using projections on the roof of the mouth. Apart from juncos, backyards also play host to white-throated and white-crowned sparrows, tree sparrows, chipping sparrows, and fox sparrows.

Doves

The mourning dove can be seen, not just in our backyards, but everywhere. It is certainly hard to miss, cooing its song from rooftops and aerials, or fluttering on to feeding platforms, scattering the smaller birds as it does so. It is one of the most productive of all our species, in some cases breeding throughout the year in one long conveyer belt of reproduction. In backyards it comes to various sorts of grain, especially corn and millet. In the north, it is migratory, and forms large flocks in the fall that are a common sight across America.

Quite recently, another species of dove, the Eurasian collared dove, has begun to get a foothold in North America, having been introduced to Florida sometime in the late 1970s. It has already reached as far north as New York and it may well expand rapidly in the next few years, as it has done in Europe from the 1930s until the present day.

Nuthatches

It's easy to identify a nuthatch; these are the birds that can scuttle down tree-trunks head-first, the only ones in the world to do so. We have two wide-ranging common species: The white-breasted nuthatch, associated with almost any kind of tree, and the red-breasted nuthatch, which has a stronger association with conifers. Both visit backyard feeders and they don't always eat a nut or seed straight away; instead they may hide it away, for instance in the cracks of tree bark, for consumption much later.

▲ Red-breasted nuthatches are common visitors to backyard feeders; their numbers may vary from year to year, according to the abundance of food supplies in the northern conifer forests.

Woodpeckers

Beginners often have difficulty separating out two common small woodpeckers—the downy and the hairy. But the downy is clearly the smaller of the two, and it has a distinctly shorter bill. The hairy is much the less frequent in city backyards, and it is more likely to be seen in leafy suburban and rural locations. Downies, though, can be found almost anywhere there are trees, and most households that provide feeding station receive regular visits from them.

Woodpeckers quickly adapt to all types of feeders, including hanging tube types, globe feeders, and even window feeders. They are particularly fond of suet, and will also take nuts of most kinds. Several species cache food in their territories for consumption later in the season.

Besides the hairy and downy woodpeckers, red-bellied woodpeckers can also be attracted to eastern backyards, although they prefer the decaying trees common to forests. Residences with large lawns can also expect visits by flickers, which feed mainly on ground ants in the breeding season, but also come for suet and fruit in the fall and winter.

American robin

The arrival of migrant American robins after the thaw, or the first hearing of the gentle, if slightly rushed song phrases of this bird in March or April, is to many people in the U.S. the most heartwarming sign of spring.

This popular species is a common sight on our lawns in the breeding season, the bird running over the grass or leaf-litter in a stop-start search for bugs in the soil. In the fall it gathers in flocks and changes its diet to fruit, and it is then that it can be a dominant species in the backyard, voraciously eating windfalls, berries, and thrown-out apples on the ground. Even so,

---

MUST KNOW

Woodpeckers

Woodpeckers are not just very welcome as residents in our backyards and woodland; they are vital components of it, too. Without the unique excavating ability of these birds, we would have many fewer chickadees, nuthatches, and bluebirds, because there would simply not be an adequate supply of holes in which to nest.

◄ A common sight feeding on lawns throughout North America, the American robin often nests on porches and ledges in buildings.

it doesn't often use feeders. Instead, despite its popularity, it keeps people at arm's length, hiding away in the shrubbery.

European starling

Never the most popular of backyard visitors, the starling is not a native North American bird at all, but was introduced to Central Park in New York City in March 1890 from Great Britain and from there spread all over the continent. It is now one of our most abundant birds. It is adapted to feeding on short grassland, using its bill to make holes in the soil and spot bugs there, but it will also come to platform feeders for suet and household scraps.

▼ European starlings will often use bird baths, but in general they are not popular backyard visitors.

Northern cardinal

The cardinal is one of those fortunate species that not only is brilliantly colored, but also makes a wonderful sound. Its mellifluous trills with their unique slurred quality are a much admired accompaniment to the suburban soundscape and, most unusually among birds, both the males and females sing. Cardinals are common visitors to backyard feeding stations, where they come for a range of seeds (including sunflowers), fruit, and peanut butter.

Raptors

One of the corollaries of feeding birds in the backyard is that they inevitably attract raptorial species. To the hunters, your feeding station is simply a fast-food outlet that it can visit again and again for reliable fare, so there is little you can do

▲ The Northern cardinal has expanded its range northward in the last 40 years or so, and it can now be found visiting bird feeders in eastern Canada.

to deter them. And if the idea of losing some of your beloved visitors is too much to bear, you might have to consider stopping feeding entirely. It is better, however, to realize that what you are seeing is natural and, in its way, both exciting and admirable.

Three species of hawks regularly prey upon backyard birds in North America. They are the sharp-shinned hawk, Cooper's hawk, and Northern goshawk. In general, the "sharpie" is the commonest and the goshawk the rarest; that might be due in part to the fact that the sharp-shinned hawk is the most specialized bird predator, the others having a broader diet.

Hummingbirds

Just about anyone who wants to bring birds into their backyard will probably have hummingbirds high on their list of requests and, happily for us, the hummers don't need much encouragement to visit. Yards can be ideal for hummingbirds if they have a sheltered environment, open aspect, and, above all, a profusion of flowers, making them a good habitat for these small birds. If you can also stand the hassle of constantly washing and replenishing their feeders, the birds will appreciate artificial feeding, and may become tame if they are fed regularly. However, hummers are irascible brutes and will frequently fight over the rights to your flowers or feeder ports.

Most households will be familiar with our most widespread species, the ruby-throated, which makes it further north than any other hummer in the world, to New Brunswick in Canada. But in the southwest the Anna's hummingbird is the commonest sight, a large (by hummer standards) species that is the only one to winter regularly in the United States. Look out, too, if you live in the Midwest for North America's smallest bird, the calliope.

▲ One of the three hawks that regularly attack birds at feeding stations, the Cooper's hawk mainly feeds on medium-sized species, such as robins and jays.

▲ Hummingbird feeders in Texas and Arizona may attract a whole range of different species.

HABITATS FOR BIRDS

Cities and urban fringes

Urban areas can often be surprisingly good for seeing a wide range of birds. Many big cities tend to have a river running through them, with some sort of embankment or even a pier, where many birds congregate.

City centers

These are often hostile places for birds, with few sources of food other than scraps which are accidentally thrown aside by people. Some city center streets attract great horned owls which feed on the mice and rats that are drawn to waste discarded around fast-food outlets, but most have only pigeons, a few European starlings, and some house sparrows, and the occasional brave house finch.

Brightly lit skyscrapers can be very dangerous indeed for birds migrating at night. Thousands of them perish when they hit windows many floors up, attracted by the lights.

Pigeons

In city centers the authorities often try to reduce pigeon (also called rock dove) numbers. Scruffy

> **MUST KNOW**
>
> **Untidy is best**
> Towns and suburbs are apt to be tidy, and open areas are often covered in short grass and ornamental shrubs—unsuitable for birds. Untidy spots with water, bushes, and rough ground can be better for birds.

▼ Although pigeons make a mess, they also add life and color to dreary city streets.

and undeniably messy, these birds add color and movement to the urban scene. Tall buildings, railroad and freeway tunnels, and even subway stations replace their natural habitat of cliffs.

▲ Birds of prey, such as this screech owl, live in our large towns and cities. They use the ledges of high buildings as safe places to roost and nest.

Raptors and owls

One city inhabitant that doesn't mind how many pigeons there are on the streets is the peregrine falcon. This impressive raptor specializes in catching and eating them, doing the former in an impressive dive from a great height, known as a stoop. The birds have made tall buildings their home, nesting on ledges with panoramic views over the pigeon-rich paradise.

Another bird of prey that does well in towns, especially the suburban neighborhoods, is the screech owl. This small species sometimes does better in manmade habitats than adjacent wild ones, feeding on the birds and small mammals that abound in suburbs and profiting from open spaces such as lawns and walkways, where they are easier to catch.

Jays and crows

American crows are canny birds that keep people at a healthy distance, while also profiting at the same time from our kitchen scraps, roadkills, and garbage dumps, and other urban trappings. They need trees in which to nest and roost, but otherwise they can enter into the most artificial environments, often patrolling empty streets early in the morning in search of scraps before there are too many people about. They are frequent visitors to backyards if encouraged but, again, they often come very early in the morning.

Blue jays, like crows, are intelligent and adaptable birds which can eat almost anything. They are famous for their ability to imitate hawks and clear the bird feeders of customers, leaving an empty tray there for the taking. They take eggs and nests of small birds in the breeding season, making them unpopular with some

▼ The American crow eats almost anything, including scraps and garbage, so it flourishes in towns and cities almost throughout the whole continent.

people. But this species is an intelligent and resourceful bird, as well as being a good-looking one. In the west it is replaced by the Steller's jay, which is slightly less adaptable than the blue, but is still a common visitor to feeding stations.

Introduced species

One ornithological surprise offered by urban America is the preponderance of introduced species that may occur there. This phenomenon is especially prevalent in the southeast and southwest, in Florida and California, where escaped cagebirds have a better change of surviving than elsewhere. Sixty-five species of parrots have been recorded as living wild in Florida alone, including significant populations of monk parakeets, which are unusual within their family for building communal stick nests.

Other introduced metropolitan species include spotted doves and common mynas, in California and Florida respectively. The latter are increasing fast, whilst the famous colony of crested mynas in Vancouver is on its last legs. But, given that house sparrows and European starlings are introduced species that have made it a bit too big here for most people's liking, all these increasing populations of naturalized birds need to be watched carefully.

▲ The Steller's jay replaces the abundant blue jay in the west. Outside the breeding season it is usually found in flocks.

HABITATS FOR BIRDS

Parks and park lakes

It is difficult to generalize about parks, because every one is different, and each has varying degrees of disturbance and different component habitats. But urban and town parks are often surprisingly good for birds and birding. Many, for example, have open areas of grass where killdeers may forage, along with grackles, cowbirds and European starlings. And almost all have lakes where wildfowl, loons, grebes, herons, and cormorants may feed, as well as numerous gulls. In the south, parks often provide a green oasis within a wide arid area, and may attract thousands of resident birds and migrants in season, including rarities. Beginners visiting their local park often bump into their first wood warblers and vireos, setting off a lifetime's passion for these fabulous birds. The value of parks should never be underestimated.

▲ We can be reminded of the wild birds living out of town, and the passing of the seasons, by flocks of geese flying overhead.

Waterbirds

A high proportion of parks have at least some open water, and these present a great opportunity to identify and learn about ducks, and offer unrivalled close views of these really attractive birds. Go in winter to see them at their best, when there will be more species present. In high summer, when the birds are molting, you will see no more than a selection of dull brown, sleepy forms. The commonest duck is, of course, the ubiquitous mallard, but you might also see black ducks.

Other waterbirds that can be seen on park lakes are Canada geese, American coots, and cormorants. The coots look like ducks at first, until you see their peculiar lobed feet, and notice that they don't have the flattened bills of ducks. You can often see cormorants on islands in lakes, resting with their wings held out to dry, as these are, surprisingly enough, waterbirds that aren't fully waterproof!

Beside the ponds, look out for herons, which often stand still at the water's edge, looking patiently in, waiting to grab anything that comes within range, be it a fish or frog or even a small mammal. And a loud rattle will announce the arrival of a belted kingfisher, a spectacular bird that catches its food by plunging into the water, either from a perch or after hovering briefly.

▼ Only the female belted kingfisher has the chestnut band on its breast and flanks. This bird is waiting silently for a fish to stir the water below.

Garbage dumps

Landfill sites can swarm with birds. Most now have strict rules and garbage is quickly buried under soil, but still large flocks of gulls, corvids, and black and turkey vultures gather around them. Each time a new load of refuse is tipped, they pile in to get what they can.

For gull enthusiasts, such places are truly wonderful—for most people, they are appalling. The noise and smell, especially in the hotter parts of the continent, are hardly appealing, and you must be careful regarding your own health and safety, and abide by access rules. It is usually best to find the field nearby where gulls rest between bouts of feeding and try to watch them there.

▼ Garbage dumps are premier places for watching and identifying gulls—but this sort of birding is only for the dedicated!

Gulls

There are few more adaptable birds anywhere in the world than gulls. They are expert at flying, swimming, or walking, and are intelligent and resourceful. In fact, gulls are adept in exploiting all manner of human trappings and have prospered as a result, being a familiar sight in towns and cities throughout North America.

They certainly have strong stomachs, visiting insalubrious places such as garbage dumps, sewage outflows, fish factories, and abattoirs to get a meal which is often far from fresh, but this does not seem to bother them. On the contrary, places like this may attract more gulls than any other local habitat, the birds crowding together in teeming, bickering flocks.

In common with their own food preferences, gulls are an acquired taste for birders. There are many species to sort out, including many that look alike, even in adult plumage, and to make matters worse, every species goes through a series of immature stages that greatly increases the identification portfolio. On the plus side, gulls are often tame and they stand still, so they make ideal study subjects for the ambitious birder.

Sewage treatment ponds

Where people are, so their waste accumulates, and therefore a sewage treatment complex will be within reach of most birders. Apart from being smelly, however, they can be surprisingly pleasant places to visit and they often teem with a wide range of birds. Shorebirds often feature, especially during migration periods, as do wildfowl. You will have to obtain permission in many cases to visit these facilities, but do try to make the effort, as it is usually worth it, and you will be rewarded with sightings of many different species of birds.

▲ The ring-billed gull is one of North America's most abundant and widespread members of the gull family.

Agricultural land

Farming in all its forms has had an enormous impact on our land. Millions of acres of forest, prairie, and wetlands have been cut down and plowed in the last couple of centuries, and this practise continues today. Other habitats, particularly grassland and prairie, are threatened by its relentless march.

Agricultural and rural areas

Land used for farming is, generally, intensively managed, and the variety of birds is reduced by the need to make agriculture or animal husbandry pay. Fields become monocultures and birds' food supplies, such as insects and plant seeds, diminish under pressure from pesticides and herbicides. But there are birds to be found, so birders should not shun these areas completely.

We still have a lot to learn about the ecology of birds in these areas, especially in the nonbreeding season. If more birders pay attention to rural bird populations, the more we can learn about them.

Widespread birds of agricultural areas include barn swallows, which often use outbuildings for nesting and hunt for flies around field edges; American kestrels hover over fields or use high

▶ Although at heart a bird of freshwater marshes, the red-winged blackbird (this is a female) is an abundant visitor to agricultural lands, especially in winter when huge flocks may form.

▲ Some birds take direct advantage of farming activities. Here, sandhill cranes are following the plow to feed on the invertebrates turned up.

perches to watch for prey below; meadowlarks spill over from their grassland habitat to seek ground-living invertebrates and seeds; horned larks gather in flocks in the winter to search for seeds on stubble or plowed fields; and bluebirds often nest close to rural homesteads.

Agricultural land is not the easiest habitat for birders—it is so open and tends to be uniform. Winter is often the best time, when birds such as sparrows form flocks to feed on seeds from fields and roadsides. But open fields do not provide much cover—for birds or birders. Flocks of foraging birds can be elusive and skittish. They need to be alert and ready to go at any moment, because predators do well on farmland.

◄ Farmland is one of the major habitats of the American kestrel.

The icterids

Many of the commonest and most noticeable farmland birds in North America, including the grackles, meadowlarks, blackbirds, and cowbirds, all belong to the same family, the *Icteridae*. With the exception of the tree-living orioles, these birds are ground foragers, and they have specially adapted bills for probing in the soil. Their muscles for opening the jaw are stronger than those used for closing it, the reverse of the usual arrangement in birds, which means that they can insert their bills and then open them whilst they are still embedded in the soil.

This means that Icterids can create holes and generally break up and shift items in the topsoil, allowing them to reach food that is unavailable to other birds. Sometimes, common grackles follow the plow instead, letting the machine do the work for them.

Sociable birds

Icterids are sociable birds. You can see flocks of them as you drive around farming areas; they seem to be everywhere—on roadsides, alongside cattle or horses in fields, on farm

▼ The Eastern meadowlark, like most Icterids, feeds on the ground and can probe its bill into the soil.

roofs, by barns. They feed by day in small or medium-sized groups, working their way across the grass like an invading army, walking or running rather than hopping, as most smaller birds do. At night red-winged blackbirds, in particular, gather in their multitudes to roost, coming to a specific favored spot from up to 50 miles around. A million or more birds may use the same roost, departing in the morning and going their various ways. One of these roosts is a spectacular sight and sound, so make an effort to find out where one is and go see it.

▼ In common with many Icterids, the breeding system of the boat-tailed grackles finds both males and females being promiscuous.

Grasslands and prairies

Grassland speaks for itself. As a habitat it can look rather disappointing for birds, and it can be difficult to work, too. However, it is more exciting and diverse than it looks, and it harbors a wide range of magnificent birds.

Grassland

Most of our grassland lies in the middle of the continent, on the Great Plains, although it can be found in a few other places as natural vegetation, and widely as the result of man's activities where brush or forest has been cut down and the resulting grassland is maintained by grazing. Many of the birds in this created grassland overlap with those that occur in agricultural land, including Icterids such as meadowlarks, grackles, and bobolinks. But natural prairies, with their specialized grassland plants adapted to a low rainfall regime, hold many species that do not occur anywhere else.

▼ The male dickcissel sings its name. Once confined to natural prairies, this species has now spread into croplands, including alfalfa.

Types of grassland

There are many different kinds of grasslands, but some distinctions are important. Some prairies, for example, have grass cover not exceeding two feet, and grow in arid areas. These short-grass prairies often attract a range of shorebirds to nest, and they have their own specialties, such as McCown's longspur.

Long-grass prairies are a different prospect; they grow in lusher areas and the grass can be taller than a man at the end of the summer growing season. The well-hidden birds of this type of habitat include Henslow's sparrow, meadowlarks, and dickcissel. Finally, intermediate between the two is the mixed-grass prairie, where the grass can grow up to three feet high.

Sparrows

The sparrows feed on grass seeds outside the breeding season, so it is hardly surprising that they are a major component of the grassland avifauna. A few, such as the lark bunting and

▼ The lark bunting nests principally on shortgrass prairie, where its fluttering song-flight is a common sight in summer.

dickcissel, are easy enough to identify, but the rest require patience and close scrutiny. The many species that exist on our continent go to prove how subtle the distinctions are between different birds' habitat. Henslow's sparrows, for example, are birds of tall grass only, while lark buntings prefer short grass, and Baird's sparrows occur in mixed-grass prairies.

▲ The choosy Henslow's sparrow likes its grassy habitat to be tall and rank, often with plenty of standing dead weeds.

Prairie-chickens and sharp-tailed grouse

Some of the most exciting birds of the prairies are the grouse. These include the sharp-tailed grouse, which occurs on various different types of grasslands, plus the lesser prairie chicken of the short-grass prairie, and the greater prairie-chicken of the long-grass prairie. These two prairies chickens, so selective in habitat, were once numerous across the plains of Central North America, but now have highly fragmented ranges. Both are endangered species.

All these grassland grouse have one special thing in common: They all form what are known as leks. These are display-ground gatherings of males. The performers join these leks at dawn and indulge in highly ritualized displays, including jumping in the air, stamping their feet against the ground, and making hooting noises with their colorful, inflatable esophageal air-sacs (purple in the sharp-tailed grouse, orange-red in the lesser prairie-chicken, and yellow-orange in the greater prairie-chicken). The aim is to sort out amongst themselves which individual is to own the central position on the lek. They are competing for high stakes, because the females, when they make their fleeting visits to the lek, will go straight to the central territory and copulate there, knowing that they have selected the best males.

Prairie potholes

In the northern Great Plains, glacial depressions filled with water dot the grassland landscape. These are excellent places for a wide range of birds, especially waterfowl, of which more breed here than in any other North American habitat. Prairie potholes are also good for California gulls and other waterbirds.

▼ Male greater prairie-chickens make their displays a communal matter, with at least eight to fifteen performers present at each lek.

Forests and woodland

Forest and woodland includes a broad range of habitat types, which essentially involve a substantial covering of trees and shrubs. Within this there is one very broad general distinction between deciduous forest (the trees of which largely shed their leaves in winter) and coniferous forest (whose needle-like leaves are retained all year), although they can be found growing together to form mixed forest. These are very broad categories, and there are many subdivisions, each with its own pool of special birds.

Coniferous forests

These forests can be subdivided according to their distribution and the climate. The main categories are: Boreal forest or taiga; mountain forest; and lowland coniferous forest.

▼ A great gray owl about to strike. This predator's hearing is so good that it can detect the movements of rodents beneath the snow.

Boreal forest

Our Boreal forest is very special. According to the National Audubon Society, it covers 1.4 billion acres, more than the Brazilian Amazon, and is the largest intact forest remaining on the planet. Although characterized by coniferous forest cover, it encompasses a mosaic of rivers, lakes, bogs, and other wetlands. About 30 percent of all the landbirds of North America breed here. It stretches from Alaska all the way across to the Canadian Maritime Provinces.

The number of species that are resident in the Boreal forest is quite small, because it can be an inhospitable place in winter. Nevertheless, several species of owl (e.g. the Northern hawk-owl, great gray owl, and Boreal owl) and some woodpeckers (black-backed, three-toed, downy, and hairy) tough it out, alongside several species of finch that specialize on cones (e.g. crossbills) or eat berries in winter (e.g. pine grosbeak). In the summer, however, the forest comes alive with an estimated two billion warblers and one billion sparrows. Typical of the warblers are the bay-breasted and blackpoll, while typical

▲ In common with several other boreal birds, the pine grosbeak is often extraordinarily tame, and will allow observers to come within a few feet as it feeds hungrily on berries.

MUST KNOW

Hard work
Birding in Boreal forests is hard work. In most areas the number of species is small compared to deciduous forests, and visiting birders can be disappointed. The best birds can be widely spaced and hard to find. So, be patient and never let your concentration waver.

▶ Occurring in many types of woodland, the ruffed grouse is the commonest member of its family in North America.

sparrows include the Lincoln's and white-throated. The sparrows are among a whole community of birds found mainly around the open, boggy parts of the Boreal zone.

Mountain forest

Also known as Cordilleran forest, this is the coniferous (and mixed) forest found at higher elevations in western North America, especially in the Rocky Mountains. It is very rich in birds and has a number of specialties, including the blue grouse, Williamson's sapsucker, Western tanager, broad-tailed hummingbird, and white-headed woodpecker.

Northwestern coastal forest

This marvelous habitat lying along the Pacific coast from California to Alaska is a type of rainforest, receiving more than 50–60 inches of rain a year. The dominant trees throughout this forest zone are Western hemlock and sitka spruce, but there are places where some of the

MUST KNOW

Bird listening
Forests are probably at their best in spring, when the birds are in their most colorful plumage and singing loudly. This habitat demands the ability to listen to and recognize bird songs. Someone with good bird song skills will detect twice as many species as someone using sight.

◀ Of our two common and widespread nuthatches, the red-breasted is the one that is most at home in conifer forests.

tallest trees in the world grow, making it a truly spectacular place to bird. If you can draw your eyes away from the impressive redwoods, you should catch sight of specialties like the delightful chestnut-backed chickadee. Other typical bird species include the red-breasted sapsucker, Townsend's warbler and, strangely, a seabird, the marbled murrelet, which nests high up in the moss-clad branches of tall trees, and may fly up to 40 miles inland after a fishing trip to feed its youngsters under cover of darkness.

Deciduous forests

South of the Boreal zone the forests take on a more deciduous flavor, although there may be plenty of conifers intermixed in places. As in the Boreal forests, the highest number of species occurs in the summer months.

Deciduous forest communities are extremely rich and even casual birders will soon become aware of how the birds use different layers, from top to bottom. For example, some birds feed mainly on the ground (e.g. the wood thrush and ovenbird), while others prefer the canopy (e.g. tanagers, orioles), and still others the shrub layer (various warblers). Some birds spend their time searching the trunks of trees, such as the brown creeper, nuthatches, woodpeckers, and black-

▲ Crossbills are nomadic birds, settling wherever they can find a good crop of pine cones, which they prise open with their crossed beaks.

and-white warbler. Others pick their food from the leaves, including vireos, chickadees, and titmice, and still others leap from a perch to make aerial sallies (including the flycatchers, waxwings, and gnatcatchers).

Birding in deciduous forests

It's not always easy birding these forests. The best plan is almost invariably to wait in one spot for a long time, preferably in an open part of the wood, and simply watch the birds come to you. In the winter the forest may appear to be lifeless at times, but this is mainly because most of the birds move around in mixed-species flocks, and their distribution is patchy.

Having spent an hour or two seeing nothing, you can suddenly find yourself overwhelmed with birds. These mixed species flocks tend to contain chickadees, titmice, nuthatches, creepers, and woodpeckers, with warblers and other migrants joining up in the fall.

Special types of forest

With all its climatic variety, it is not surprising that North America has a wide range of different wooded habitats, each dominated by one or two key tree species. Many of these have their own characteristic bird communities, and they include the following.

• **Oak woodlands** Found mainly in the southwest, these support such species as acorn, Nuttall's, and Arizona woodpeckers, plus the oak titmouse.

• **Pinyon-juniper** Another community of the southwest, also with its own specialized titmouse, the juniper titmouse. The pinyon jay, an arch storer of food, is also characteristic of this type of forest.

• **Pine-oak forest** An important but declining habitat of the southeast that grows on sandy, well-drained soils. Characteristic birds are the brown-headed nuthatch, red-cockaded woodpecker, chuck-will's-widow, and Mississippi kite.

Forest edge and shrubland

Shrubland is the name often given for the plant community midway between grassland and forest. Dominated by trees that are smaller than those found in the forest, and usually encompassing open areas, it may arise in two ways. It can be a step on the way to woodland, or it can be a stable community in its own right, the prevailing rainfall being too low for forest, but not too low for trees and shrubs. It often arises when a patch of ground is cleared, for agriculture, is then abandoned and begins to regenerate; on its journey to becoming forest, the vegetation is shrubby.

Although synonymous with disturbance and easily regarded as a second-class habitat, shrubland is very good for birds, both breeding species and migrants. It supports plenty of food and safe nesting sites. Among the many species that use shrubland are the yellow-billed and black-billed cuckoos (perhaps because these birds have a taste for hairy caterpillars), the Northern bobwhite, catbirds and thrashers, and a host of skulking warblers including the yellow-breasted chat.

▲ It can be difficult to spot a black-billed cuckoo as it moves stealthily around amidst thick cover.

MUST KNOW

Chaparral

Chaparral is a type of shrubland found along the west coast from California to south Oregon, characterized by plants with waxy leaves and often an aromatic smell. Thriving under hot summers and rainfall of 15–40 inches per year, and maintained by periodic fire, chaparral supports many bird species, including California quail, Bewick's wren and spotted towhee. To many, though, the wrentit is the chaparral bird, its marble-dropping call being the habitat's most distinctive voice.

Deserts and arid areas

A broad section of the southwest of North America is arid enough country to be called desert. It is characterized by having too little rain to support much plant growth, and has wild fluctuations in temperature between day and night. It makes for a harsh environment in which to live, but a surprisingly wide variety of birds do occur.

Types of desert

There are various types of desert in North America, each supporting slightly different birdlife. The most widely accepted system lists four main categories, although some experts put the number much higher, up to 20. The best known is the Sonoran Desert of California and Arizona, with its landscapes dominated by the celebrated, candelabra-shaped saguaro cactus. Holes in these cacti are used by the world's smallest owl, the elf owl, and the region supports a range of other special birds of various kinds, including several species of woodpeckers, cactus wren, Harris's hawk, hummingbirds, and the greater roadrunner.

Roadrunners

The roadrunner does exist, although there are a few differences in reality from the cartoon character. For one thing, roadrunners don't go "Beep, beep"; they make dove-like cooing noises.

This is a well adapted bird of the desert, which shows a number of physiological and behavioral traits to go with its way of life. To combat extreme heat by day it can cool itself down by evaporating water from its skin, pant like a dog and expose the pale feathers below its wings to reflect the heat. It saves water by reabsorbing moisture from the lower intestine and removing salt through its nasal glands.

WATCH OUT!

Desert birding
This should not be undertaken lightly, or it can be fatal. Make sure you have enough water with you, more than you think you will need. Wear a hat at all times. Don't exert yourself. Take a mobile phone and a GPS. Come prepared for a car breakdown. The best times for birding are also the most comfortable times for you—early morning and evening. Whereas the desert morning chorus can be something to remember, night birding is also good.

To combat the cold at night, the roadrunner reduces its own body temperature in order to use less energy, and then warms itself up for a while in the morning sun, a bit like a reptile.

Talking of reptiles, these are very much a part of the roadrunner's wide diet, and remarkably this includes rattlesnakes. The birds are able to run back and forth in confrontation with a rattler and eventually gat a grip on the back of the reptile's head. Once secured, the roadrunner strikes the snake's head and body repeatedly on a hard surface.

▲ The greater roadrunner is one of the easiest desert birds to see because, as its name suggests, it can often be seen running along roads and tracks. At full pace, it can run at 15mph.

The sleeping one

There is only one bird in the world that is known to hibernate, and that is the poorwill of the deserts of the southwest. This species can enter into a torpid state for months on end during the winter, maintaining its body temperature at a remarkably low 18°C. No other bird comes close to being torpid for that length of time, although many hummingbirds will become torpid overnight, and some bird chicks for a few days. Remarkably this obscure behavior was known to the Hopi Indians whose folk name for the bird was "the sleeping one."

Tundra

The tundra is not a single habitat but a mosaic of landscapes found north of the 10°C summer isotherm—i.e. where the average summer temperature is 10°C or less. Tree growth is not possible here, and the lower soil is permanently frozen.

▼ The inhospitable tundra is only suitable for birds for a few months each year.

Summer in the tundra

For a short period in summer, the tundra comes alive. The snow disappears. The ice in the top layer of soil melts, creating a patchwork of pools and lakes. The Arctic plants grow and flower and create a habitat for a superabundance of insects. This change makes the tundra suddenly capable

of supporting millions of birds. For as little as six weeks in the summer, the Alaskan and Canadian tundra is a breeding ground for two main groups of birds: Waterfowl, including geese, and shorebirds. There are also a few hardy smaller birds, such as longspurs, buntings, and pipits.

The shorebirds primarily eat insects and insect larvae, a somewhat different diet to what we are used to seeing down south, when many of the same birds are probing the mud for worms and shellfish. The young ducks, and many of the adults, too, will also eat bugs.

Another "boom" product in the tundra is small mammals, primarily voles and lemmings, and a significant proportion of tundra birds, including jaegers, hawks, and owls depend on them. These rodents have cycles of population, which may mean they are everywhere one year, but scarce the next, and the breeding success of the rodent-eating predators is affected in kind.

▲ One of the many shorebirds nesting in the tundra, the Hudsonian godwit winters in southern South America.

The toughest of the tough

Remarkably, a few birds can eke out a living permanently in the tundra. The rock ptarmigan, for example, may occur at 83° north in Greenland. It does this by eating what seems like the most extraordinarily bland food, subsisting for months on end on just willow and birch twigs. These are easy to find, and there is little competition for them. The ptarmigan's gut is large and long, enabling it to extract every drop of nutriment from its unpromising fare.

A suitable diet is not all it needs, but special adaptations against the cold, too. All the ptarmigans have feathered legs and feet, and even their nostrils are feathered. They also have thick, multi-layered plumage, which changes in color according to the state of the tundra landscape—white for winter, mottled brown for the breeding season.

MUST KNOW

Fast breeders
The boom of summer is short-lived, and may be over in the northernmost part of the tundra in less than 100 days. This means that some birds have to take active measures to speed up production. Brants, for example, fatten up prior to their arrival so that they can be on-site before the frost melts and food becomes available to them.

Mountains

Mountains provide a great birding habitat, not so much because they are high but because they tend to be unsuitable for agriculture and have historically been left reasonably intact. Some of the quietest and least disturbed parts of the continent lie within mountain ranges.

Mountain birds

A few birds are specialists of the high tops of mountains, where the climate does not allow trees to grow. These include tundra specialists like the gray-crowned rosy finch, which often takes insects direct from snowfields as they are immobilized by the cold, and the white-tailed ptarmigan, which, like its relatives in the Arctic tundra, eats shoots and twigs in the winter, and is one of the few species to sit out the entire winter season at high altitude.

Most other mountain birds are found in the forests that cloak the lower slopes. A few species are characteristic of rocky slopes and cliffs, including the rock wren and white-throated swift, and some are found on mountainside brush, such as the mountain quail.

▼ One of the few North American birds found only on mountain tundra, the white-tailed ptarmigan can be found as high as 14,000 feet in the Rockies.

Common ravens

These are exceptionally widespread birds in the Northern Hemisphere, ranging from the Arctic to hot deserts. They nest on cliff ledges and in big trees, laying very early when the weather is still harsh and often incubating their eggs during falls of snow. They are tough, dramatic birds, easily located if you recognize their loud, resonant, deep-throated call-notes.

▲ Ravens are massive, black crows, whose beautiful, resonant calls echo around cliffs and mountain peaks.

MUST KNOW

Mountain hiking

This is an exhilarating pastime but you will see few birds and some of the most exciting only at long range. Never take mountains lightly—they can be dangerous places, where the weather is liable to change quickly and catch out the unwary, and an encounter with a dangerous mammal, such as a bear or mountain lion, is possible. Use the right footwear and clothing, and take food and drink, good maps, and a compass or GPS. Tell people where you are going and when you expect to get back.

Lakes and rivers

Even non-birders know that freshwater lakes can be great places for birders, because birds are so visible. Shallow, productive waters may teem with ducks, grebes, loons, shorebirds, herons, egrets, and so on.

Water birds

Lakes offer a birder the chance to appreciate some of the subtleties of bird ecology. How do so many birds fit into one habitat? What are they eating? Some, such as mergansers, cormorants, and loons, eat fish; others, such as coots and some ducks, eat pondweed and vegetation; others, including the smaller grebes, eat aquatic invertebrates. They get their food in different ways and from different places. Herons and egrets fish the shallows; mergansers swim and dive in the middle; and kingfishers plunge in from the edge.

Even within the same group there may be many different feeding strategies. Some ducks dive while others feed only from the surface. Some prefer to up-end (pintail), others to dip only their heads in (gadwall), or keep their bill on the surface, dabbling (Northern shoveler). Some, like the wigeon, prefer not to be in the water at all, but instead graze along the edges.

▼ With its long neck, the Northern pintail can reach down deeper into the water in search of food than other non-diving ducks.

American coots

These have a weakness in their feeding system. They graze vegetation on the lake bottom, but they are so buoyant that they always return to the surface before swallowing it. This enables certain ducks, including gadwalls and American wigeons, to sneak in and steal it from them when they come up. And, despite being highly aggressive, the smaller coots have no answer to this thieving behavior.

Reading a lake

You can tell quite a lot about a lake by the birds on it. If the ducks present are primarily surface-feeding (or "dabbling") ducks, you can be sure that it is quite shallow. If the birds are primarily diving ducks (except ruddy ducks), you can guess that the water is six feet or more deep. Certain ducks are indicators of fresh water, as opposed to brackish or saline, including the gadwall and Northern shoveler.

▲ Loons, like this Pacific loon, are found on deeper lakes which are stocked with plenty of large fish.

MUST KNOW

Reservoirs

Reservoirs mimic natural lakes but have a greater tendency for dramatic changes in level: a rise in spring may flood out nesting birds, while a fall in late summer and autumn can create perfect conditions for migrant shorebirds, seeking wet or dried mud on which to feed.

Rivers

These develop from the smallest, clear mountain stream to a broad or mighty watercourse, heavy with silt, approaching an estuary or delta. So they are difficult to categorize as a single habitat. Nevertheless, there are some birds for whom that most consistent of a river's characteristics, its flow, is the most important. These include two extreme specialists, the American dipper (page 120) and the harlequin duck.

The harlequin lives in rapids and cascades, feeding on shellfish, crustaceans, and insect larvae that it pulls off rocks while diving. The heavily oxygenated water provides plenty of food for this remarkable duck, so all it has to do is fight against the current and rest from time to time on the slippery rocks. Yet so completely is it adapted to its habitat that birds have been known to nest behind waterfalls. In the fall, it moves downriver and seeks out rough, rocky coasts, the sort of place that makes it feel at home.

▲ The harlequin duck is one species that depends on the flowing nature of rivers.

◄ Mallards can be found almost anywhere there is water, but they also fly to feed on fields at night, far away from their daytime wetland roost.

Waterthrushes

The Northern waterthrush and the Louisiana waterthrush are delightful members of the wood warbler family that have become waterside foragers. They walk along the water's edge, head-bobbing, and turn over leaves and other fragments to reveal what's underneath. The two species have slightly different habitats, the Louisiana waterthrush preferring flowing water, the Northern often content with still water.

Bald eagle

A great wildlife spectacle is the gathering of bald eagles at the Chilkat River in Alaska to feed on the run of chum salmon. The birds may number up to 4000 in their mid-November peak and come from many miles around to feast on this unusual late season abundance caused by upwellings of warm water in the river, keeping fish available long after other rivers have frozen. It is such a meeting place that the area has been dubbed the Bald Eagle Council Grounds.

▲ The waterthrushes are unusual warblers that feed mainly on the ground in damp places. The Louisiana waterthrush is mainly confined to flowing watercourses.

▼ The bald eagle has the taste for fine fish.

Coasts and islands

North America has a massively long coastline, and many parts are exceptionally rich in coastal birds. Habitats vary enormously from muddy estuaries to vast deltas, and from open sandy bays to sheer cliffs; from mangroves in the south to Arctic shores and bays in the north.

Estuarine environment

As a river reaches the sea, it widens and deposits its load of silt in an estuary or delta. Incoming tides swirl around the mouth of the estuary and build up a network of sand and shingle. Behind this a saltmarsh builds up: Thick mud dissected by innumerable creeks and overgrown with salt-tolerant plants. In some places there are sand-dunes, stabilized by other special plants, with low-lying dune slacks just inland where shallow pools are rich in flower and insect life.

▼ Black-bellied plovers and smaller dunlins are great travelers, breeding right up into the Arctic, but relying on estuaries and similar muddy habitats for survival in the fall and winter.

The whole complex of such an estuarine environment can be full of birds. Sandy and shingle-covered areas will provide habitat for snowy or even piping plovers, together with colonies of gulls and terns, from the gull-sized Caspian tern to the diminutive least tern. The mouth of the estuary can attract seaducks such as eiders, oldsquaws, and scoters, plus American oystercatchers, turnstones, and surfbirds if there are rocks and seaweed.

From early fall to spring the rich mud can teem with shorebirds, including godwits, willet, semipalmated and Western sandpipers, dunlins, dowitchers, black-bellied and semipalmated plovers, and red knots, depending on the location. The mud here is so rich that it can support literally thousands of edible organisms for every square yard.

Nearby, there will always be gulls. North America is very rich in these, and both coasts have their own special species: Laughing gulls and great black-backed gulls in the east and Heerman's, Western, and glaucous-winged on the west coast. Somehow they all eke out a separate living without merging into one species.

▲ The scoters are ducks that, when not breeding, are primarily found on the coast. This distinctive bird is a male Surf Scoter.

▼ The large, predatory glaucous gull is found mainly in the far north.

Aleutian Islands
These 200 or so islands in the Bering Sea, between Alaska and Russia, are home to some of North America's largest seabird colonies. Several species occur nowhere else in the world. Specialties include red-legged kittiwake, whiskered auklet, least auklet, and crested auklet. They are one of North America's great wilderness areas.

Cliffs and islands

Some parts of North America have cliffs lining the shore, rather than a low-lying coastline, and these provide breeding opportunities for countless millions of nesting birds. The great thing about cliffs is that they are inaccessible to ground predators, but to birds, with wings, they are no problem at all. We have cliffs on both sides of the continent, each with their own special communities of birds.

On the Atlantic side there are many fewer species than in the west, and most are confined to the north-eastern tip of the continent. They

▶ Vast colonies of seabirds on sheer coastal cliffs provide some of the most dramatic spectacles in our wildlife. Seabirds are among our finest treasures.

include the highly sought-after Atlantic puffin, the Northern gannet, black-legged kittiwake, and northern fulmar, among others. Each of these species commutes from the breeding ledges to hunt for fish or marine invertebrates at sea. Puffins, razorbills, and murres dive underwater, gannets make spectacular plunge dives, sometimes from 100 feet up; kittiwakes usually snap fish from the surface and fulmars grab food while swimming on the surface.

The Pacific coast teems with one of the specialty families of sea cliffs, the alcids, or auks. The various species all dive for their food, sometimes up to 600 feet down, using their wings to power them underwater. The various species feed at different depths, in different states of the current, and on different food. The murres, for example, take fish; the auklets take planktonic crustaceans, and the weird parakeet auklet uses its curved bill to munch jellyfish.

▲ Black-legged kittiwakes breed on sheer cliffs on both sides of the continent.

Pelagic

The true seabirds are those that generally do not come close to the shore, but feed over the deep waters of the true ocean. You can watch these birds in two ways. One is to let the birds be blown toward you, and the other is for you to join the birds on the oceans.

The former method of allowing the birds to be blown toward you is known as seawatching. It tends to involve a long sit with a spotting scope, usually fairly high up, scanning the sea from the land. It is highly unpredictable but, not surprisingly, is most successful after a long blow inshore. Hurricanes, for instance, often bring some oceanic birds within range of the coast, but it need not be this drastic. Seawatching is great for birders when it goes well and very boring when it doesn't. Take plenty of time and employ a lot of patience.

▼ Crested auklets breed mainly on the Aleutian Islands, but they are also occasionally seen from the coast of Alaska.

Pelagic trips

Birders can go on to the water themselves by joining what are known as pelagic trips. The aim of these trips is to take a boat out to where the water is very deep, beyond the continental shelf. In some parts of North America this actually lies surprisingly close inshore, notably in Monterey Bay, California, and the trips from here are among the most successful anywhere.

These trips can often last for quite a number of hours, and the birds that you see are hard to predict from one outing to the next, but for the chance of seeing shearwaters, storm petrels, albatrosses, and alcids, they offer complete joy for seabird nuts. Obviously, pelagic trips are not for the faint of stomach. If you suffer from seasickness, you're asking for trouble, although you can take some medication before setting out to help guard against this.

▲ Shearwaters, such as these Audubon's shearwaters, are difficult to see from land, and it may require a pelagic trip to get them on to your lifelist.

Marshes and swamps

Marshes can be thought of as wetlands that are mainly covered in vegetation rather than having open water, though in practice there will usually be some of both in the same system. Water can be in the region of one through three feet deep. These habitats tend to be seasonally rich in birds, very active in spring and summer but quieter in winter, although there may be plenty of resident species, too.

Marshland birds

These birds live in dense, often tall-stemmed vegetation. The small birds of marshes, such as marsh wrens, need strong legs and feet for grasping vertical stems, and are often highly agile. Rails are highly adapted marshland birds with laterally flattened bodies, squeezed at the sides. They have long toes to spread their weight over the mud, preventing them sinking.

Most marsh birds are very noisy, producing loud songs that make up for the fact that they cannot see their colleagues through the tall vegetation. These sounds are often heard at dawn and dusk, and they may offer the only evidence that a particular species is present.

MUST KNOW

Mating
A high proportion of marshland birds have mating systems in which males pair with several females at a time. These include the red-winged, tricolored and yellow-headed blackbird, the American bittern, and the marsh wren.

◄ The marsh wren has a distinctive and loud song.

► The American bittern is usually a difficult bird to find, but it sometimes leaves the safety of marshland vegetation to hunt out in the open.

Many marsh birds are highly secretive; the yellow rail, for example, can usually only be seen when a group of people walk shoulder to shoulder through a marsh in a deliberate effort to flush one, as if they were cops combing the ground for clues. Marsh birding is for the patient.

Swamps

Swamps are wetlands dominated by trees, with permanent water below the trunks. There are various types in North America, including the cypress swamps of the south, with protruding tree roots and clumps of Spanish moss, and the red maple swamps of the north. Ducks that

▼ The strange limpkin—not quite a heron, a rail, or a crane, and in a family of its own—feeds mainly on large snails.

▲ The sora is quite a common bird, but most people have hardly ever seen one because of its secretive habits.

breed in holes in trees, such as wood ducks and buffleheads, not surprisingly do well in swamps. So do a number of woodpeckers, some warblers (notably prothonotary), wood storks, and limpkins.

Ivory-billed woodpecker

Just about every birder in North America has grown up resigned to the fact that the ivory-billed woodpecker was extinct, a victim of persecution and the reduction of its bottomland habitat. Then, sensationally, in 2004, the bird was rediscovered after a 50-year gap in the Big Woods region of Arkansas. To date there have been a handful of sightings and a very brief clip of video footage. But that is evidence enough that, just occasionally, miracles happen in birding.

want to know **more?**

Take it to the next level...

Go to...
▶ **Getting involved** page 178
▶ **Need to know more?** page 188

Other sources
▶ **The North American Bird Conservation Initiative (NABCI)**
   for information on bird conservation
▶ **The American Birding Association**
   for finding out more about seabirds
▶ **Internet**
   for information on conservation surveys
▶ **Birding clubs**
   for meeting other birders
▶ **Publications**
   visit www.buteobooks.com for bird books

getting

involved

Once you are set up as a birder, with your fieldguide, binoculars, and your favorite places to visit, you might want to get more involved with some other birders, a bird club or a conservation organization; it's up to you. Birding has the great benefit of being the easiest, cheapest, and least regulated pastime that you can possibly imagine.

Take it one step further

Birding may be just an enjoyable hobby for you, and that's great if so. You may spend years enjoying backyard birds and leave it at that. Birding has no rules, and you should just enjoy it. Attracting birds to your backyard is one way to develop your hobby that benefits the birds as well. However, you can take it further and give it a purpose.

Getting more out of it

Backyard birds give us a lifetime's enjoyment, but you might want to take your birding interest further, to get a little more out of it. Getting more out generally means putting more in, and there might be more paperwork and correspondence. If you move into conservation matters, you might find yourself feeling angry, depressed, or even helpless, or you may get great satisfaction and joy out of winning a fight for the birds.

Rarely does the birder assess these things in advance. Birding takes you into places you've never been before, in so many ways. You may not be a campaigner until a developer threatens your favorite birding location; or you may be

◄ Vacations open up a new world of birds. In much of southern and central Europe the hoopoe is one of the more exotic looking species that you might never get a chance of seeing at home.

inspired to help a particular species that means something to you. Then you go into battle, and good luck to you.

Extend your horizons

Not all birders wish to, or can afford to, travel, but getting to a new habitat, or to a different region, is still the simplest way to see more birds than you can observe close to home.

Vacation birding

Vacations offer huge opportunities for spotting new or unfamiliar birds. The birds of the United States are so varied that a relatively short plane journey or a longer road trip can bring you into places that are inhabited by a very different set of birds to those you are used to, and you can use the same fieldguide. Birding guidebooks have been written for almost every U.S. state and these will tell you exactly where to look and

▲ Some of the most popular places for birding vacations are in the southern states, where the best birds draw the galleries!

Vacations

Keep records of the birds you see when you are on vacation. The ones you take in more remote places, where there are few birdwatchers about, can add more useful information than a whole year spent in a familiar area.

▼ Soon coming to your neighborhood? The advance of the collared dove is being carefully monitored in the U.S.

what to look for. In most areas you can meet up with the local Audubon Society, or even hire a personal guide to help you.

Further afield the birding gets even more challenging, especially if you take a leap into the species-rich melting pot of South America. Europe may be a better bet, especially since many of the birds there are comparable with those back home.

Use your records

Some birders are sociable and quickly join groups of people with the same interest; others prefer to bird alone and find species for themselves. Whichever category you belong to, it's good to share your records and let others know what birds can be seen where. If, for example, you know of a good birding site in your neighborhood, you might miss an opportunity to protect it from development if you keep your observations to yourself. At present there are several ways in which you can make your records and sightings contribute to the science of ornithology in North

America. Further details on these Citizen Science programs are available at www.birdsource.org.

eBird

This is a continent-wide year-round survey of North American birds. Providing you have internet access, you can log in details of any sightings you make anywhere, anytime, and compare them to those of others. This program also stores information on birding sites.

Christmas Bird Count

One of the great traditions of North American birding, this survey has been going for over 100 years, a period of study unparalleled in the world. It is run by the National Audubon Society. Participants go out for a day of counting every bird in their allotted area, around the Christmas period. It's hard work but great fun, and every birder should do it.

The Great Backyard Bird Count

This survey is run over a specific four-day period, in which participants count every bird they see at their feeders or on a walk of less than a mile anywhere they like. It is easy to submit the records online. It just makes your Christmas bird trips contribute to a continent-wide database.

Project Feederwatch

This is a project that runs from November through early April. Participants count the birds using their feeders on two consecutive days every two weeks. You can spend the whole day watching if you like, and you record the highest number of individuals of a certain species you can see at the same time. You can submit your records online. This is a very absorbing survey, best done by quite committed backyard birders.

▲ Try to attract birds such as the Baltimore oriole to your backyard, so that you can participate in doing a count. Get involved with the North American Breeding Bird Survey to help track changes in North American bird populations.

Your local area

A great way to develop your birding is to find a "local patch."
This does not have to exclude birding in other places; you
can still get about as much as you like. However, if you have
a place where you can go for half an hour before or after
work, in your lunch break, or after school, this can be really
useful and relaxing. If you can get there at the weekend and
put in the hours then, too, you are really blessed.

Become an expert

You might even become the local expert—the
one person who knows more than anyone else
about the birds of this special place. Keep notes,
make sketch-maps, write lists, and take notes of
the other wildlife in the area. Send your records
to a national database and put the place on the
birding map.

Don't neglect well-known places that already
seem well covered; they may not be. A local
state park, wildlife refuge, or trail may attract
many birders, but still not have a "regular" who
knows the place inside out. Why not become
that regular? It could be very rewarding.

▶ If you watch birds as
often as you can at a
specific locale, such as
a local park or lake, you
can become "the expert"
on its birdlife. Even if there
is nothing rare, you will
get great satisfaction from
knowing all about the birds
that can be seen.

Finding rarities

You might never see any rarities. But, if after five
years, you see a field sparrow for the first time,
you know how good that is—anything new might
become unusual and exciting. If you watch an
area time after time, one day you will discover
something genuinely unexpected and rare, and
then you will know how satisfying it is to find it
yourself, instead of following the news on the
Rare Bird Alert. A rarity demands discipline. You
must watch it for as long as you can. Take notes,
describe it, draw it, photograph it, and let others
go see it, too.

Joining a club

There are hundreds of bird clubs all over the U.S. and Canada, from small ones that concentrate on one wetland, wildlife refuge, or county, to big ones with thousands of members. So if you would like to learn more and share your knowledge and enthusiasm with other birders, go ahead and join a club. Check the internet for groups in your area and beyond.

Why join?

Once you join you will probably receive regular newsletters and, perhaps for a few more dollars, an annual report. There will be regular field visits that you can join and indoor meetings to attend. Here you can learn more about birds, places to watch birds, and the people who see them. Birding can be a solitary pursuit, which is best done quietly, with minimal disturbance. However, being excited by birds is best enjoyed with a companion. Nothing beats saying to a fellow birder, "Did you see that?" with feeling. Turning around, elated by a magnificent sight, to find no-one there can be deflating.

Share your experiences

So, if you want a birding buddy, join a club. If you just want to talk about birds, join a club. You may learn a lot, or you may teach a lot. Share your experiences, ask questions, talk birds and birding. It all helps to develop your hobby and will take you into new areas—photography, bird banding, writing, or finding new publications and specialist books.

MUST KNOW

Club benefits
Local bird clubs will benefit birders of all levels of experience. If you are a beginner, you will learn more; if you are experienced, you can help others. The best are friendly organizations from which everyone will benefit. Make sure you get the most out of your club: Attend meetings, write to the newsletter editor, and take advantage of the benefits it provides.

▶ The Aplomado falcon.

Need to know more?

A wealth of further information is available for birdwatchers, particularly if you have access to the internet. Listed below are some useful organizations and resources.

National societies

Smithsonian National Zoological Park: Birds
3001 Connecticut Avenue NW
Washington, DC 20008
http://nationalzoo.si.edu/Animals/Birds/
default.cfm

Smithsonian Ornithology
http://sio.si.edu/

Smithsonian Migratory Bird Center at The National Zoo
http://nationalzoo.si.edu/ConservationAnd
Science/MigratoryBirds/

American Birding Association, Inc.
P.O. Box 6599, Colorado Springs,
CO 80934–6599
tel: (800) 850–2473/(719) 578–9703
email: member@aba.org
http://www.americanbirding.org/index.html

The American Ornithologists' Union
Suite 402
1313 Dolley Madison Blvd
McLean, VA 22101
http://www.aou.org/

Cornell Lab of Ornithology
http://www.birds.cornell.edu/

National Audubon Society
700 Broadway
New York, NY 10003
tel: (212) 979-3000
http://www.audubon.org/

North American Rare Bird Alert
Sponsored by the Houston
Audubon Society
440 Wilchester Blvd.
Houston, Texas 77079
http://www.narba.org/default.htm

Ornithological Societies of North America
OSNA Business Office
5400 Bosque Blvd Ste 680
Waco, TX 76710
tel: (254) 399-9636
http://www.osnabirds.org

US Environmental Protection Agency: Bird Conservation
Ariel Rios Building,
1200 Pennsylvania Avenue,
N.W. Washington, DC 20460
tel: (202) 272-0167
http://www.epa.gov/owow/birds/

US Fish and Wildlife Service Office of Bird Management
Headquarters: 1849 C Street,
N.W. Washington, DC 20242
http://www.fws.gov/birds/

Wild Birds Unlimited, Inc.
Franchise Support Center
11711 N. College Ave,
Suite 146, Carmel, IN 46032
tel: (317) 571-7100
http://www.wbu.com/

Magazines

Birder's World Magazine
Kalmbach Publishing Co.
21027 Crossroads Circle P.O. Box 1612
Waukesha, WI 53187
http://www.birdersworld.com/

Birdwatcher's Digest Magazine
http://www.birdwatchersdigest.com/site/
index.aspx

Online resources

Birding.com
www.birding.com

Birdwatching.com
www.birdwatching.com

Birdsource
www.birdsource.org

National Bird Feeding Society
"Helping create bird-friendly backyards"
http://www.birdfeeding.org/

Smithsonian Environmental Research
Center, Avian Ecology Lab
http://www.serc.si.edu/labs/avian/index.jsp

Equipment

In Focus
tel: 800-294-6400
www.infocus.com

Bushnell
tel: 800-423-3537
www.bushnell.com/index_us.cfm

Eagle Optics
tel: 800-289-1132
www.eagleoptics.com

Eastern Mountain Sports
tel: 888-463-6367
www.ems.com

Leica
tel: 800-222-0118
www.leica-camera.com

Orion Telescopes and Binoculars
tel: 800-447-1001
www.telescope.com

Nikon
www.nikon.com

Swarovski
www.swarovskioptik.com

Zeiss
www.zeiss.com

Food & feeders

Bird and Yard
http://www.birdandyard.com/

Duncraft
www.duncraft.com/index.ihtml

PRD Seed
www.prdseed.com

Lyric Wild Bird Food
http://www.lyricbirdfood.com/

Wagners
http://www.wagners.com/home.html

Vacations

Birdquest
www.birdquest.co.uk

Field Guide Birding Tours Worldwide
www.fieldguides.com

Focus on Nature Tours
www.focusonnature.com

Bibliography

Kaufman, Ken, et al., *City Birding*
(Stackpole Books)

Kaufman, Ken, *Kaufman Field Guide
to Birds of North America*
(Houghton Mifflin)

Kaufman, Ken, *Lives of North American
Birds* (Peterson Natural History
Companions, Houghton Mifflin)

*National Audubon Society Field Guide
to North American Birds: Eastern
Region* (Knopf)

*National Audubon Society Field Guide
to North American Birds: Western
Region* (Knopf)

Peterson, Roger Tory, *A Field Guide
to the Birds of Eastern and Central
North America* (Houghton Mifflin)

Peterson, Roger Tory, *A Field Guide
to Western Birds* (Houghton Mifflin)

Sibley, David Allen, *Sibley's Birding
Basics* (Knopf)

Sibley, David Allen, *Sibley's Guide
to Birds* (Knopf)

Glossary of terms

Bill: The same as beak—an extension of the jaws with a horny sheath.

Breeding plumage: The brightest plumage at a time when birds display, find mates, and defend a territory.

Breeding season: The period of the year when birds nest, lay eggs, and rear their young.

Brood: A set of young birds reared at one time, from one clutch of eggs.

Clutch: A set of eggs incubated by a sitting bird.

Colony: A group of nests close together.

Flock: A group of birds, acting to some extent in concert.

Habitat: The characteristics of a bird's environment, including the flora and fauna, soils, water, climate, and altitude.

Incubation: Maintaining even temperature of an egg, by sitting (brooding), so the embryo develops and hatches.

Migration: Regular seasonal movement of bird populations.

Nest: A receptacle for eggs and, in some cases, chicks.

Pair: A male and female, together for the purpose of breeding—a basic unit used in counting the numbers of birds.

Passage migrant: A bird that neither breeds nor winters in an area but may be seen in spring and fall.

Plumage: The covering of feathers. Also different age, season or sexual variations in appearance of plumage.

Preening: Caring for the feathers by drawing each one through the bill to maintain its shape and structure; also to add oil from the preen gland to keep the feathers waterproof.

Roost: To sleep; a place where a bird sleeps; a group of birds sleeping or resting together.

Territory: An area of ground defended by one bird, or a pair, or a family group, against others of the same species for the purpose of nesting (and providing food) or, outside the breeding season, for feeding.

Vocalization: A "call" (or call note), used for keeping contact, warning of predators, begging for food; or a "song," used by males (sometimes females) to help proclaim and defend a territory and attract a mate.

Acknowledgements

The following photographs are reproduced courtesy of rspb-images.com:
Niall Benvie: p. 48; Nigel Blake: p. 102; David Broadbent: pp. 21, 178; Richard Brooks: pp. 55, 133, 170; Peter Cairns: p. 62; Bob Glover: pp. 35, 54, 66; Chris Gomersall: p. 142; Michael Gore: p. 49; Mark Hamblin: pp. 17, 60; Andy Hay: pp. 3, 14, 20, 22, 30, 91, 107, 116, 163, 168; Barry Hughes: p. 67; Malcolm Hunt: pp. 15, 18, 63; Ernie Janes: pp. 32, 46, 124; David Kjaer: p. 19; Steve Knell: pp. 72, 156; Chris Knights: p. 115; Mike Lane: p. 180; Gordon Langsbury: pp. 58, 59, 82; George McCarthy: p. 106; Phillip Newman: p. 52; Roger Wilmshurst: p. 107
FLPA: pp. 2, 51, 65, 75, 118, 119, 126, 138, 151, 152, 169, 171, 172, 173, 182
Mike Read: pp. 1, 11, 12, 23, 27, 34, 36, 38, 42, 44, 50, 57, 68, 69, 70, 77, 78, 79, 81, 84, 86, 88, 93, 95, 96, 98, 101, 103, 104, 109, 110, 111, 113, 114, 120, 122, 125, 128, 129, 130, 131, 133, 134, 135, 137, 141, 143, 144, 145, 154, 155, 157, 159, 164, 166, 169, 175, 181, 187
David Tipling/davidtipling.com: pp. 2, 3, 7, 8, 29, 33, 40, 53, 56, 57, 61, 69, 74, 76, 77, 79, 80, 83, 85, 87, 89, 90, 94, 97, 100, 108, 114, 139, 146, 147, 148, 149, 150, 153, 160, 161, 162, 165, 166, 167, 174, 176, 177, 183, 185

Index

Numerals in italics refer to illustrations